CREDITS AND CONTRIBUTORS

We thank the following for their invaluable help in the compilation and publication of this book.

The Siteman Family Foundation
The Missouri History Museum
The St. Louis Post-Dispatch

THE MUNY ARCHIVISTS

Stephen Guebert
Patty Ackerman
Jon Barrientos
Jane Bastien
JoAnn Berger
Judi Boles
Suzanne Corbett
Marcy Cornfeld
George Durnell
Peggy Garcia
Beth Going
Barbara Labitska
Michael Leonardelli
Sarah Luedloff
Ray Martin
Audrey Monahan
Dan Monahan
Diane Neske
Andrew Sherwin
Debbie Smith
Dave Sprecker
Kathy Waeltermann
Tom Wethington
Don Wilhelm
Dick Wobbe

THANK YOU TO

Jay Traxel
The Scottish Rite, Valley of St. Louis
Sharon Smith,
Missouri History Museum

CONTRIBUTING AUTHORS

"St. Louis' Fabulous Municipal Theatre:
Fifty Seasons of Summer Musicals"
by Charles V. Clifford

"The Muny: St. Louis' Outdoor Theater"
by Mary Kimbrough

"Curtain Time in Forest Park"
by Marvin Holderness

Judith Newmark,
Theatre Critic St. Louis Post-Dispatch
Ron Elz
Suzanne Corbett

DESIGN, PHOTOGRAPHY AND EDITING ASSISTANCE

Stephen Guebert
Jon Barrientos
Joy Boland
Judy Sakai
Dylan Stanley

ST. LOUIS SHOWBIZ BEFORE THE MUNY

St. Louis has long been a city that loves music and theatre. We boast of the second oldest symphony orchestra in the country, and of course, The Muny is America's oldest and largest outdoor musical theatre.

Prior to The Muny, Yiddish, German, and Polish theatres, vaudeville houses and movie theatres flourished. Uhrig's Cave, located in mid-town, was St. Louis' first "air-conditioned" theatre, and audiences flocked to see Sarah Bernhardt and other notable actors of the day perform there. The earliest production of *The Mikado* was performed at Uhrig's in 1885, although it was a "pirated" version.

THE REPERTORY BEFORE THE MUNY
1916-1918

Once the space had been delineated and proven to be a fine area for civic events, more shows, pageants and concerts were scheduled there. Below is a list of those events, from the first production on that site [*As You Like It*] leading up to the first season of the Municipal Theatre Association.

Pre-Muny entertainment in St. Louis centered around "the flickers," vaudeville, live theatre, and musical concerts.

1916

As You Like It	(June 5 - 12)
Pied Piper of Hamelin	(September 1)

1917

Aida	(June 5 - 9)
Masonic Celebration	(June 30)
Navy League Celebration	(July 4)
Pagliacci	(July 20 - 30)
Fashion Pageant	(August 13 - 22)
Rip Van Winkle – Playground Festival	(August 30)
Pageant Choral Chorus	(September 17)

1918

Greek Games, Central High School	(May 28 - June 1)
Concert, Art League	(June 8)
Red Cross Performance, YWCA	(June 10)
Fighting for Freedom	(July 4 - 7)
Fashion Pageant	(August 5 - 6, 12 - 13, 19 - 20)
Robin Hood – Playground Festival	(August 29)

1919

Greek Games, Central High School	(May 24)
Victory Pageant, Women's Council of St. Louis	(May 31)
Flag Day, Elks	(June 14)

LEFT: Program cover from 1918 *Independence Day Pageant*

RIGHT: An ad from the 1923 *Fashion Pageant* program

The Pageant and Masque, 1914

In celebration of the 150th anniversary of the founding of St. Louis, an elaborate Pageant and Masque were created. They were held at the Grand Basin near Art Hill, and are credited as being a major influence on the subsequent founding of The Muny.

GREATEST CROWDS SINCE FAIR HERE FOR THE PAGEANT

Fifteen Thousand Visitors Pass Into City at Union Station and Many Arrive at McKinley Terminal and Washington Avenue for Four Days' Celebration.

St. Louis Post-Dispatch, May 28, 1914

From the Missouri Historical Society Collections

WHAT IS A PAGEANT?

A large scale entertainment consisting of performers in elaborate, colorful costumes forming a parade, or an outdoor performance of a historical scene.

WHAT IS A MASQUE?

An allegorical dramatic entertainment, the style originating in the 16th and 17th centuries, sometimes performed by masked performers representing abstract ideals or concepts.

From the St. Louis Post-Dispatch

From the Missouri Historical Society Collections

The Pageant and Masque was played by a cast of 7,500 upon a vast stage that was built over the Grand Lagoon at the base of Art Hill. The pageant depicted the story of the city's early years, beginning with the Mound Builders and concluding with the end of the Civil War.

As You Like It 1916

From The Muny Archive

1916 marked the tercentenary of Shakespeare's death, and the city of St. Louis sought a special way to celebrate. It was decided that an *al fresco* presentation of *As You Like It* would be presented in Forest Park. A New York stage actress, Margaret Walsh Anglin, was hired to act as producer and director of the show, and to perform the role of Rosalind.

Photo by Martin Schweig

"On Sunday, November 21, 1915, Miss Anglin...visited Forest Park...When she was taken to the site of the open-air theatre, she was delighted. Miss Anglin tested the acoustics by speaking from the proposed stage, while [others] listened from the hilltop. It was found that every word could be heard clearly."

From "St. Louis' Fabulous Municipal Theatre"
Charles V. Clifford.

NOTABLE CAST MEMBERS

SYDNEY GREENSTREET, as Touchstone
Greenstreet began his career as a stage actor, and did not make a film until the age of 62. He is best known for his work in movies with Humphrey Bogart, most notably as the Fat Man in *The Maltese Falcon* (1941) and Signor Ferrari in *Casablanca* (1942).

LOUIS CALHERN, as Sylvins and Shepherd
Calhern enjoyed a prolific stage career, but it was his work at MGM that made him known. He appeared in *Duck Soup* with the Marx Brothers (1933), as Uncle Willie in 1940's *The Philadelphia Story* and concluded his career as Buffalo Bill in the 1950 film *Annie Get Your Gun*.

ALFRED LUNT, as LeBeau
A stage actor and director, Lunt's career is closely tied to that of his wife's, Lynn Fontanne. The Lunt-Fontanne Theatre on Broadway is named for them.

MARGARET ANGLIN

3

PLAYGROUND PAGEANTS

Beginning around 1913 and continuing sporadically into the early '40s, The Muny hosted a post-season event for young people. Playgrounds around the city would organize neighborhood children and rehearse specific scenes from a pre-selected show. Then, in late August, all would come together at The Muny and perform the piece *in toto*. Later in the history of these Pageants, a "Festival" was added, including games and treats for the children donated by local merchants.

Below is a partial listing of Playground Pageants from 1913 through 1937. These were performed at the site of today's Muny.

Sleeping Beauty	1913
The Pied Piper of Hamelin	August 31, 1916
Rip Van Winkle	August 30, 1917
Rip Van Winkle (Repeat Performance)	Sept. 13, 1917
Robin Hood	August 29, 1918
Hansel and Gretel	1919
Little Red Riding Hood	Sept. 1, 1920
Ali Baba and the Forty Robbers	1921
Snow White and the Seven Dwarfs	1922
Aladdin and the Wonderful Lamp	August 29, 1923
The Pied Piper of Hamelin	August 28, 1928
The Goose Girl	1934
The Quest of the Harlequin and the Columbine	August 31, 1937

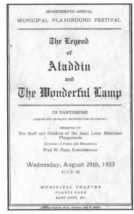

Program cover from
Aladdin,
Playground Pageant,
1923

From The Muny Archive

An early incarnation of
The Muny Kids?

From The Muny Archive

Fashion Pageants
1917 - 1924

About The Fashion Pageant

"In August [1917] the amphitheatre was used for a different purpose, [a fashion show]...The St. Louis Style Show Committee contributed funds toward the construction of the playhouse with the understanding that its Fall Festival and Fashion Pageant would be given there later in the summer. It was due to the success of its first pageant, which had been presented at the Moolah Temple in February, 1917, that the organization had money to pledge to the project in the park. There were semiannual shows again in 1918 (the spring event being at the Odeon Theatre), but after that they were only held once a year."

From "St. Louis' Fabulous Municipal Theatre"
Charles V. Clifford

Photos by Martin Schweig Photography

Program pages on this and opposite page from the 1923 Fashion Pageant.
From The Muny Archive

AIDA, 1917

In preparation for the for the Associated Advertising Clubs of the World's convention slated for early June, it was decided that "a spectacular production of *Aida* [would] be given." The site of today's Muny, which had proved to be so satisfactory for the previous year's *As You Like It,* would be ideal.

OPEN-AIR THEATER READY IN 40 DAYS, CUNLIFF PROMISES

Army of Workmen and Teams Active in Preparation for Production of "Aida."

St. Louis Post-Dispatch, Sunday, April 22, 1917

"Commisioner Cunliff of Parks and Recreation...announced that from April 19 it would require 42 days to complete the work as plotted.

"There are 50 men and 15 teams working on the grading and the form building of this immense theater. Workers began pouring concrete Friday. It will take 27 days to complete this task in the auditorium."

SNAPSHOTS

The photo at RIGHT shows the newly-finished auditorium and stage, with the ballet from *Aida* rehearsing. BELOW RIGHT, an unidentified cast member posing backstage.
BELOW: The men and teams preparing the auditorium for the opening of *Aida*.

From The Muny Archive

Photo colorization by Dan Monahan. Image from The Muny Archive

From The Muny Archive

AIDA, 1917

THE STORY IN A PHOTO
BY ANDREW HAHN

Photo courtesy of
The Campbell House Museum, St. Louis, MO

"Hidden in the voluminous archive of the Campbell House Museum is a photo taken in the summer of 1917 of The Muny stage set for its first production of the opera *Aida*. The back of the photo tells an interesting story. It bears the inscription, 'To Mr. Hugh Campbell, from Tamro Yamajo. The Open Air Theatre. This picture was taken with the camera you presented me. Excellent. The Art Museum in the background over the forest.'

"A well-known patron of the arts and photography, Hugh Campbell (1847-1931) met Yamajo and gifted him with a camera. Yamajo in turn gave Campbell one of his first photos taken with the camera. The photo, along with thousands of other objects, including letters, furniture and carriages have been preserved at the Campbell House ever since."

Andrew H. Hahn
Executive Director
Campbell House Museum

OFFICIAL
LIBRETTO PROGRAMME
PRICE 18 CENTS

INAUGURAL OF THE
MUNICIPAL THEATRE
Forest Park, June 5 to 9, 1917
SPECTACULAR PAGEANT PERFORMANCES OF
« AIDA »

SAINT LOUIS GRAND   CONVENTION BOARD
OPERA COMMITTEE   ADVERTISING CLUB OF ST. LOUIS

THE PROGRAM

The program cover from *Aida,* 1917

THE REVIEW

The World Advertising Federation convened in St. Louis and in Forest Park for Verdi's *Aida*. The consensus of opinon from the audience, the press, and the sponsors was uniformly positive.

Prominent Persons Give Great Praise to Recent Performance of "Aida"

Inaugural of St. Louis' Open-Air Theater in Forest Park Made Lasting Impression on Visiting Advertising Men.

From the St. Louis Globe-Democrat

Muny Firsts, 1919

The Repertory, 1919

Robin Hood	(June 16 - 21)
The Bohemian Girl	(June 23 - 28)
El Capitan	(June 30 - July 5)
The Mikado	(July 7 - 12)
The Wizard of the Nile	(July 14 - 19)
The Chimes of Normandy	(July 21 - 26)

In the first season, The Muny ran from Monday through Saturday, with each operetta playing for six performances.

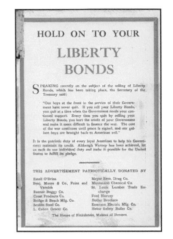

The First Muny Brochure

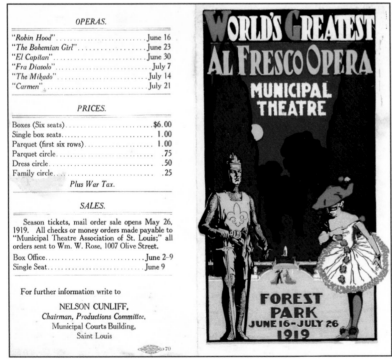

OPERAS.

"Robin Hood"	June 16
"The Bohemian Girl"	June 23
"El Capitan"	June 30
"Fra Diavolo"	July 7
"The Mikado"	July 14
"Carmen"	July 21

PRICES.

Boxes (Six seats)	$6.00
Single box seats	1.00
Parquet (first six rows)	1.00
Parquet circle	.75
Dress circle	.50
Family circle	.25

Plus War Tax.

SALES.

Season tickets, mail order sale opens May 26, 1919. All checks or money orders made payable to "Municipal Theatre Association of St. Louis;" all orders sent to Wm. W. Rose, 1007 Olive Street.

Box Office	June 2–9
Single Seat	June 9

For further information write to

NELSON CUNLIFF,
Chairman, Productions Committee,
Municipal Courts Building,
Saint Louis

From the Missouri Historical Society Collections

NOTE: Two shows originally scheduled and listed in the brochure, *Fra Diavolo* and *Carmen*, were replaced by *The Wizard of the Nile* and *The Chimes of Normandy*.

The First Muny Survey

From the Missouri Historical Society Collections

GREATEST HITS OF THE 1910S

C1919
A photo of one of the very first Muny audiences.

1919
An image from *Robin Hood*, in its first outing at The Muny.

C1919
A Playground Pageant performance, undated, but judging by the undeveloped features of the stage, very likely to have been *Hansel and Gretel*.

AMERICA IN THE 1920S

- Average life expectancy for men was 53.5 years.
- Fuel for cars was only sold in drug stores.
- Only 14% of homes had a bathtub.
- Only 8% of homes had a telephone.
- The maximum speed limit in most cities was 10 mph.
- The tallest structure in the world was the Eiffel Tower.
- The average US wage in 1910 was 22 cents / hour.
- The average US worker made between $200 and $300 per year.
- More than 95% of all births took place at home.
- Eggs were 14 cents a dozen.
- Coffee was 15 cents a pound.
- Most women only washed their hair once a month.
- The population of Las Vegas, Nevada was 30.
- Two out of every 10 adults could not read or write.
- Only 6% of all Americans had graduated from high school.
- Marijuana, heroin and morphine were all available over the counter at local drugstores.
- There were about 230 reported murders in the entire United States.

STATE OF THE MUNY
THE MUNICIPAL OPERA HAS BECOME CITY FAD
St. Louis, June 21, 1924 (Special)

"In all my journeying about America, in my travels through Europe, I have seen nothing to be compared with this," [Actor Walter Whiteside] said, looking on the chorus of 100 St. Louis boys and girls, in the beautiful revival of *Florodora*.

"Why, this is an institution. It should be patterned after by every city in America. You will remember Zangwill's play, *The Melting Pot*, well this is St. Louis' melting pot. I've been watching the people as they passed in aisle before me... Everybody here seemed to know most everybody and everybody had a personal interest, it seemed, in the cast and the success of the performance...

"I look around here. Everybody's out for a good time. For enjoyment. They are not even concerned about the fascinating task of setting the stage which is going on like clockwork back of those lights...What an inspiration!"

From The St. Louis Post-Dispatch
June 21, 1924

ANNOUNCEMENT

*f*OR the comfort of its patrons, the Municipal Theatre Association has arranged to furnish, at the small rental of ten cents for each performance, clean, comfortable cushions. They may be procured at the main entrances or through the courtesy of ushers. LOVE'S PATENTED CUSHIONS with clothes protector attached, to cover back of chair, used exclusively.

MADE ENTIRELY NEW FOR THIS SEASON

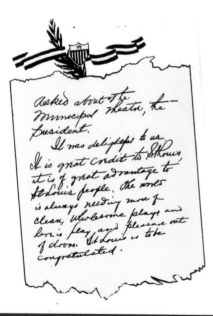

From the 1927 program

The above ad featured movie theatres, vaudeville houses, and combinations of the two.

PRESIDENT HARDING AND
THE PRINCE OF PILSEN, 1923

President and Mrs. Warren G. Harding attended a production of *The Prince of Pilsen* on June 23, 1923. Although scheduled to stay only through the first act, Mrs. Harding did not want to leave, and they watched the entire production. When asked for his impressions of The Muny, Harding said: "It was delightful to us. It is great credit to St. Louis, it is of great advantage to St. Louis people. The world is always needing more of clean, wholesome plays, and here is play and pleasure out of doors. St. Louis is to be congratulated."

"Six weeks later, Mayor Henry W. Kiel announced from the same stage that the President had died in San Francisco. The performance of *The Spring Maid* was cancelled, and the stunned cast and audience left the theatre."

Mary Kimbrough

REPERTORY

1920S

1920

The Firefly	(June 8 - 13)
Robin Hood	(June 15 - 20)
A Waltz Dream	(June 22 - 27)
The Mikado	(June 29 - July 4)
The Mascot	(July 6 - 11)
The Gondoliers	(July 13 - 18)
Babes in Toyland	(July 20 - 25)
Katinka	(July 27 - August 1)

1921

The Chocolate Soldier	(June 7 - 12)
Fra Diavolo	(June 14 - 19)
The Fortune Teller	(June 21 - 26)
San Toy	(June 28 - July 3)
The Beggar Student	(July 5 - 10)
The Pirates of Penzance	(July 12 - 17)
The Chimes of Normandy	(July 19 - 24)
Sari	(July 26 - 31)

1922

The Highwayman	(June 6 - 11)
Sweethearts	(June 13 - 18)
Sari	(June 20 - 25)
The Yeoman of the Guard	(June 27 - July 2)
The Geisha	(July 4 - 9)
The Spring Maid	(July 11 - 16)
The Queen's Lace Handkerchief	(July 18 - 23)
Miss Springtime	(July 25 - 30)

NOTE: From 1920 - 1922, each show ran for six performances, from Tuesday through Sunday.

1923

Naughty Marietta	(May 28 – June 3)
Wang	(June 4 - 10)
The Fencing Master	(June 11 - 17)
The Prince of Pilsen	(June 18 - 24)
Die Fledermaus	(June 25 – July 1)
Sweethearts	(July 2 - 8)
The Gypsy Baron	(July 9 - 15)
The Merry Widow	(July 16 - 22)
Gypsy Love	(July 23 - 29)
The Spring Maid	(July 30 – August 5)

1924

Princess Chic	(May 26 – June 1)
The Firefly	(June 2 - 8)
Florodora	(June 9 - 15)
The Chinese Honeymoon	(June 16 - 22)
The Bohemian Girl	(June 23 - 29)
The Prince of Pilsen	(June 30 - July 6)
The Fortune Teller	(July 7 - 13)
The Lilac Domino	(July 14 - 20)
Naughty Marietta	(July 21 - 27)
The Beggar Princess	(July 28 - August 3)

1925

A Night in Venice	(May 25 - 31)
M'lle Modiste	(June 1 - 7)
Ruddigore	(June 8 - 14)
Her Regiment	(June 15 - 21)
Rob Roy	(June 22 - 28)
Dolly Varden	(June 29 – July 5)
Erminie	(July 6 - 12)
Cavalleria Rusticana/ H.M.S. Pinafore	(July 13 - 19)
The Count of Luxembourg	(July 20 - 26)
Martha	(July 27 - August 2)
Naughty Marietta	(August 3 - 9)
The Merry Widow	(August 10 - 16)

REPERTORY

1920s

1926

Eileen	(May 31 - June 6)
The Red Mill	(June 7 - 13)
The Chocolate Soldier	(June 14 - 20)
The Spring Maid	(June 21 - 27)
The Pink Lady	(June 28 - July 4)
Il Trovatore	(July 5 - 11)
Sweethearts	(July 12 - 18)
Iolanthe	(July 19 - 25)
The Count of Luxembourg	(July 26 - August 1)
Woodland	(August 2 - 8)
Fra Diavolo	(August 9 - 15)
Babes in Toyland	(August 16 - 22)

1927

Robin Hood	(June 6 - 12)
The Princess Pat	(June 13 - 19)
Sari	(June 20 - 26)
The Song of the Flame	(June 27 - July 3)
The Red Mill	(July 4 - 10)
Rose Marie	(July 11 - 17)
The Mikado	(July 18 - 24)
The Dollar Princess	(July 25 - 31)
Katinka	(August 1 - 7)
The Serenade	(August 8 - 14)
Gypsy Love	(August 15 - 21)
The Tales of Hoffman	(August 22 - 28)

1928

Princess Flavia	(June 4 - 10)
The Merry Widow	(June 11 - 17)
The Vagabond King	(June 18 - 24)
No, No, Nanette	(June 25 - July 1)
Rose Marie	(July 2 - 8)
The Student Prince	(July 9 - 15)
The Lady in Ermine	(July 16 - 22)
The Song of the Flame	(July 23 - 29)
Countess Maritza	(July 30 - August 5)
The Love Song	(August 6 - 12)
Mary	(August 13 - 19)
Aida	(August 20 -26)

1929

The Love Call	(June 3 - 9)
The Student Prince	(June 10 - 16)
Wildflower	(June 17 - 23)
Castles in the Air	(June 24 - 30)
The Chocolate Soldier	(July 1 - 7)
The Bohemian Girl	(July 8 - 14)
Rose Marie	(July 15 - 21)
The Prince of Pilsen	(July 22 - 28)
The Enchantress	(July 29 - August 4)
The Vagabond King	(August 5 - 11)
Babes in Toyland	(August 12 - 18)
Golden Dawn	(August 19 - 25)

Score from the collection of Robert Sorrells

BEAUTIFUL MUSIC

At right is the score of *The Firefly,* first performed at The Muny in 1920. *The Firefly* was also produced there in 1924, '39, '41, '45 and '49.

BLINDERS

From The Muny Archive

The Muny stagehands had a crafty way of changing the scenery without the audience seeing: A row of bright lights lined the orchestra pit, and when turned on, created a blinding "curtain of light." This allowed the sets to be changed without the audience seeing the magic happen.

Close-up of "blinders."

Press releases referred to this strategy as "the light curtain," but the term "blinders" is what has held through the years.

THE DORIC COLUMNS,

1919 - 1920

From The Muny Archive

The Doric columns that line the back of the theatre were completed in 1920. This early postcard clearly shows those columns.

From the Missouri Historical Society Collections

The photo ABOVE shows star and director of *As You Like It* Margaret Anglin, who returned to The Muny in 1919 in order to plant a tree for Arbor Day. Behind her, one can see the Doric columns, back by the free seats, as a work in progress.

SOUND AMPLIFICATION

Robin Hood, 1927. Photo by A.W. Sanders

In 1922, The Muny Board of Directors approved $12,000 for the equipment and labor for their installation. The five bullhorns stretched over the stage represented state-of-the-art sound amplification. The work was done by the Western Electric Company.

STARS OF THE 1920S

DOROTHY MAYNARD
Dorothy Maynard was a Muny leading lady between 1923 and 1926. She starred in 23 shows in those years.

WALTER WHEATLEY
Walter Wheatley appeared only once in Forest Park. In 1925, Wheatley played Turridu in *Cavalleria Rusticana*.

Photos above were digitally process from glass plate negatives found in The Muny Archive.

LUCKY LINDY AND PRINCESS PAT, 1927

Shortly after Charles Lindbergh's transatlantic flight, he made a Muny appearance. 12,000 people gathered to greet the hero, and The Muny reported an evening's take of $7,000 – "the largest amount of money ever taken in at the theater at any scale of prices." It was reported that Lindbergh stayed for the first act of *The Princess Pat*, and left at intermission.

___ ST. LOUIS POST-DISPATCH ___

Lindbergh, Weary, Dreading Footlights, Flees Opera

Permits Himself to Be Led to Stage, Bows Slightly and Retreats Out of Theater to Host's Home

FLORODORA

1924

In their day, a Florodora Girl in the cast of the New York hit was as glamorous as a Ziegfeld beauty. The Muny continued a tradition that began in New York, when they double cast the Florodora Sextette with a children's chorus. Their song, "Tell Me, Pretty Maiden," was the stand-out number of the operetta.

The 1924 sextette from *Florodora*. From The Muny Archive

From The Muny Archive

The use of a children's sextette continued in 1933 with the second (and last) Muny production of *Florodora*.

THE MUNY CHORUS SCHOOL

RIGHT: The Muny sponsored a chorus school in the 1920s, designed to prepare talented St. Louisans for The Muny ensemble. The qualifications for that program were outlined in a 1922 press release.

MUNICIPAL OPERA CHORUS TRAINING SCHOOL -- 1925.

All applicants to be not under 16 years of age.

Residents of St. Louis Missouri, also St. Louis County, Missouri.

Sopranos, Altos, Tenors, Basses.

To devote four evenings each week to the training school.

To be taught sight reading in Music, ensemble singing, dramatic and stage training including characterization.

Those showing qualifications will be give special courses toward their development in playing parts.

Those passing qualifications will be chosen for a special all chorus school production of a selected opera to be presented as a compliment to the chorus school at some local theatre prior to the regular opera season.

This daytime shot shows the stage and setting for *The Mikado*, 1920.

This nighttime image of *The Chimes of Normandy,* 1921, shows a scene lit for dramatic effect.

Elaborate sets and large choruses were the hallmark of Muny operettas in the '20s. *The Chocolate Soldier*, 1921

All photos on this page from The Muny Archive

THE 1930S

AMERICA IN THE 1930S

- Average life expectancy for men was 58.1 years.
- Average cost of a gallon of gas was 10 cents.
- Average cost for a loaf of bread was 9 cents.
- Average cost for a new home was $3,845.
- Average cost of a new car was $600.
- Average annual wage was $1,970.
- At the height of the Great Depression, gangster Al Capone opened a soup kitchen.
- In response to the wave of suicides inspired by the Stock Market Crash, hotel clerks were rumored to have asked guests checking in if they wanted a room for "sleeping, or for jumping."
- In 1934, the jobless rate was at 25%.
- Hostess Twinkies, Snickers, and sliced Wonder Bread were introduced.
- Penicillin, Scotch tape, chocolate chips, frozen foods, and nylon stockings were invented.
- Atom splitting, the Loch Ness monster and the planet Pluto were discovered.

STATE OF THE MUNY

"The Opera had passed through the panic of 1929 and '30 with no casualties and but few scars.

"Up to that point, the Opera had operated as a kind of stock company, but now the Board of Directors decided to step out, and get a professional producer of the Broadway or Metropolitan Opera type. The idea was to stage each show in much the same way as the Broadway shows, except to make sure the staging maintained all advantages of their outdoor theatre with its natural, sylvan beauty."

By Marvin E. Holderness
From *Curtain Time in Forest Park*

THIS SHIFT, WHICH BECAME KNOWN AS "THE TRANSITION," SIGNALED A MAJOR TURNING POINT IN THE MUNY'S EVOLUTION.

THE MUNY DECLARES ITSELF "DEPRESSION PROOF"

St. Louis, May
"St. Louis believes its far-famed Municipal Opera is depression proof. As result, with a repertory which includes three world premieres, six other works new to its stage and three glorious revivals of operetta masterpieces it is undertaking a program which is of international significance in its fifteenth season, to open in the Municipal Theatre, Forest Park, Monday, June 5."

Three World-Premieres to Mark Municipal Opera's 15th Anniversary Season

St. Louis to Hear Latest Viennese Operetta by Franz Lehar, for First Time on Any Stage.

St. Louis, May — St. Louis believes its far-famed Municipal Opera is depression proof. As result, with a repertory which includes three world premieres, six other works new to its stage and three glorious revivals of operetta masterpieces it is undertaking a program which, is of international significance in its fifteenth season, to open in the Municipal Theatre, Forest Park, Monday, June 5.

1933 Press Release

REPERTORY

1930s

1930

Nina Rosa	(May 30 - June 8)
The Circus Princess	(June 9 - 15)
The Desert Song	(June 16 - 22)
The New Moon	(June 23 - 29)
Blossom Time	(June 30 - July 6)
Alone At Last	(July 7 - 13)
The Red Robe	(July 14 - 20)
Maytime	(July 21 - 27)
Madame Pompadour	(July 28 - 3)
The Student Prince	(August 4 - 10)
Show Boat	(August 11 - 24)

1931

Three Little Girls	(May 29 - June 7)
The Street Singer	(June 8 - 14)
Music in May	(June 15 - 21)
Nina Rosa	(June 22 - 28)
Rose Marie	(June 29 - July 5)
Countess Maritza	(July 6 - 12)
The Three Musketeers	(July 13 - 19)
A Wonderful Night	(July 20 - 26)
Irene	(July 27 - August 2)
The Circus Princess	(August 3 - 9)
Rio Rita	(August 10 - 23)

1932

The New Moon	(June 6 - 12)
The Riviera Girl	(June 13 - 19)
The Last Waltz	(June 20 - 26)
Blossom Time	(June 27 -July 3)
The Desert Song	(July 4 - 10)
Rose of Stamboul	(July 11 - 17)
The Honeymooners	(July 18 - 24)
The Blue Paradise	(July 25 - 31)
Sari	(August 1 - 7)
The Land of Smiles	(August 8 - 14)
The Love Call	(August 15 - 21)
Cyrano deBergerac	(August 22 -28)

1933

Bitter Sweet	(June 5 - 11)
Florodora	(June 12 - 18)
White Lilacs	(June 19 - 25)
Rip Van Winkle	(June 26 - July 2)
Nina Rosa	(July 3 - 9)
The Student Prince	(July 10 - 16)
The Nightingale	(July 17 - 23)
Naughty Marietta	(July 24 - 30)
My Maryland	(July 31 - 6)
Beau Brummell	(August 7 - 13)
The Cat and the Fiddle	(August 14 - 20)
The Desert Song	(August 21 - 27)

1934

Sweet Adeline	(June 4 - 10)
Sweethearts	(June 11 - 17)
Cyrano deBergerac	(June 18 - 24)
The Last Waltz	(June 25 - July 1)
East Wind	(July 2 - 8)
Mlle. Modiste	(July 9 - 15)
Music in the Air	(July 16 -22)
Rose of Algeria	(July 23 - 29)
Sally	(July 30 - August 5)
The New Moon	(August 6 - 12)
Show Boat	(August 13 - 26)

1935

Teresina	(June 3 - 9)
Rio Rita	(June 10 - 16)
Madame Sherry	(June 17 - 23)
The Chocolate Soldier	(June 24 - 30)
Good News	(July 1 - 7)
The Vagabond King	(July 8 - 14)
Sunny	(July 15 - 21)≠
The Beloved Rogue	(July 22 - 28)
The Cat and the Fiddle	(July 29 - August 4)
The Desert Song	(August 5 - 11)
Roberta	(August 12 - 18)
Whoopee	(August 19 - 25)

REPERTORY
1930S

1936

Kid Boots	(June 5 - 14)
The Three Musketeers	(June 15 - 21)
No, No, Nanette	(June 22 - 28)
Sons O'Guns	(June 29 - July 5)
The Bohemian Girl	(July 6 - 12)
Oh, Boy!	(July 13 - 19)
The Merry Widow	(July 20 - 26)
The New Moon	(July 27 - August 2)
A Connecticut Yankee	(August 3 - 9)
Bitter Sweet	(August 10 - 16)
The Red Mill	(August 17 - 23)
Glamorous Night	(August 24 - 30)

1937

The Great Waltz	(June 4 - 13)
The Fortune Teller	(June 14 - 20)
Music in the Air	(June 21 - 27)
Louie the 14th	(June 28 - 4)
The Mikado	(July 5 - 11)
Salute to Spring	(July 12 - 18)
The Prince of Pilsen	(July 19 - 25)
The Bartered Bride	(July 26 - August 1)
The Pink Lady	(August 2 - 8)
Robin Hood	(August 9 - 15)
Babes in Toyland	(August 16 - 22)
Wild Violets	(August 23 - 29)

1938

Gentlemen Unafraid	(June 3 - 12)
Of Thee I Sing	(June 13 - 19)
White Horse Inn	(June 20 - 26)
Roberta	(June 27 - July 3)
Virginia	(July 4 - 10)
Lost Waltz	(July 11 - 17)
The Chimes of Normandy	(July 18 - 24)
Rosalie	(July 25 - 31)
Knights of Song	(August 1 - 7)
The Gingerbread Man	(August 8 - 14)
Show Boat	(August 15 - 28)

1939

Rose Marie	(June 2 - 11)
Queen High	(June 12 - 18)
Lost Waltz	(June 19 - 25)
Katinka	(June 26 - July 2)
A Waltz Dream	(July 3 - 9)
On Your Toes	(July 10 - 16)
The Firefly	(July 17 - 23)
The Bartered Bride	(July 24 - 30)
Mary	(July 31 - August 6)
Babette	(August 7 - 13)
The Song of the Flame	(August 14 - 20)
Victoria and Her Hussar	(August 21 - 27)

Ads from the 1935 program

Show Boat
1930

Photo by Ruth Cunliff Russell

The History of Show Boat

Show Boat debuted on Broadway in 1927 and the Shuberts brought it to Forest Park in 1930. Since then, the show has enjoyed a total of 15 productions at The Muny. It is the only show in The Muny's repertory that has been produced every decade since its 1930 incarnation.

W.C. Fields
The Muny's First "Cap'n Andy"
By Brad Holiday

From The Muny Archive

When Fields played The Muny in 1930, he was already a Ziegfeld star, and famous for his quick-witted ad-libs. It seems that he decided to skip a rehearsal on an unusually hot summer day, and a group of actors sought him out at his hotel.

"There they found him...looking disheveled in his old bathrobe, and contentedly practicing his golf swing by driving cotton balls into the drapes.

"'Out, intruders!' he shouted, adding a typical touch of Fields wit with, 'Unless you plan to play through!'"

By Brad Holiday, St. Louis Journals, March 16, 1988

Brad Holiday was a St. Louis performer, who appeared at The Muny 22 times between 1966 and 1991.

The Muny, Harry Fender & Mr. Ziegfeld

In 1926, St. Louisan Harry Fender was working for the great Ziegfeld in New York. "Ziggy" was preparing to open Edna Ferber's *Show Boat*, and wanted Fender to play Gaylord Ravenal. Fender pled illness, fled the country and began a game of hide-and-seek with Mr. Ziegfeld.

Eventually, Fender moved back to St. Louis, and joined the police force. He retired in 1946, became the host of a live radio show on KMOX, and played Captain 11 on Channel 11. In the 1990s, he was "the Voice of The Muny," recording the pre-show anthem announcements. He made one Muny stage appearance, as Silk 'At 'Arry in *Oliver!* (1976).

CARY GRANT, Actor
1931

Archie Leach began his show business career as a stilt walker and Vaudeville performer while still in England. He toured the U.S. in the early '20s, eventually moving here. He had done several shows in New York under the auspices of the Shubert brothers, who hired him to perform at The Muny for its 1931 season. In seven of the 11 shows produced that year, he was cast as the resident baritone. Leach did not return to New York at the end of that summer, but moved to Hollywood, where he quickly made a name for himself as one of cinema's most popular and enduring leading men. Among his most notable films are *Charade, North by Northwest*, and *The Bishop's Wife*.

Who's the tallest, tannest, most handsome man in the crowd? Standing fifth from the left is Archie Leach, in a casual cast shot.

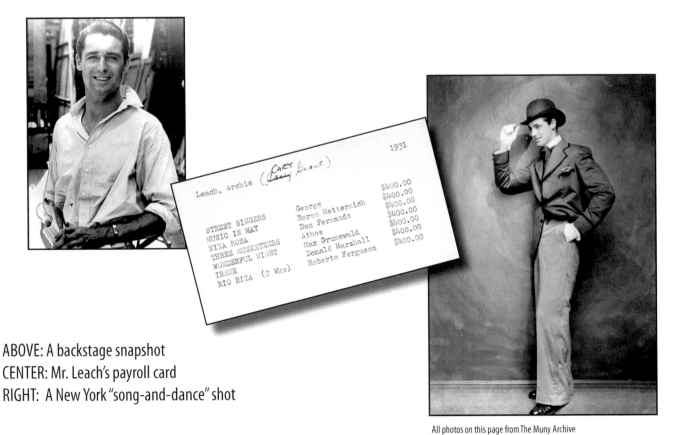

ABOVE: A backstage snapshot
CENTER: Mr. Leach's payroll card
RIGHT: A New York "song-and-dance" shot

All photos on this page from The Muny Archive

THE SHUBERTS

In 1930, the Board of Directors brought in Milton Shubert as productions director. As such, he would be responsible for both the stage and musical directors. This alliance with the Shuberts, the Board reasoned, would give The Muny access to resources the Shuberts could provide: props and costumes, popular show titles, New York directors, and actors with the names and the talents to sell tickets. Milton served as The Muny's producer for only one year, 1930, and he was followed by his uncle, J.J. Shubert, who produced at The Muny from 1931 through 1934.

MILTON SHUBERT

J.J. SHUBERT

LAURENCE SCHWAB

"When Laurence Schwab, (who had collaborated on the books for such successes as *The New Moon, Queen's High, Good News* and *Follow Through*) became general production manager at the opera in 1935, he completely abandoned the semi-stock company which had been used by the Shuberts since 1930. Under his system, stars who were especially suited for their specific roles appeared on a weekly basis."

Charles V. Clifford

RICHARD BERGER

Richard Berger followed Laurence Schwab as The Muny's general production manager, and served in that position from 1937 through 1943. He began his Muny tenure as an assistant to Schwab, and left for a career in Hollywood. Berger brought some of the most distinguished stage performers of their day to Forest Park, but one of his greatest discoveries was Jacob Schwartzdorf.

JACOB SCHWARTZDORF
AKA JAY BLACKTON

Jacob Schwartzdorf music directed and conducted at The Muny from 1937 through 1943. Oscar Hammerstein met him at The Muny during rehearsals for *Gentlemen Unafraid* in 1938. When Hammerstein teamed up with Richard Rodgers for their first Broadway collaboration, *Oklahoma!*, they enlisted Schwartzdorf to conduct. Jacob changed his name to Jay Blackton, became one of New York and Hollywood's most sought after musicians, and earned an Academy Award for scoring *Guys and Dolls*.

All photos on this page from The Muny Archive

UNDER CONSTRUCTION

THE TURNTABLE, 1930

One of the first innovations introduced by Milton Shubert in 1930 was the turntable. The Muny Board voted to approve $10,000 for combined costs of the turntable and upgraded lightning equipment.

From The Muny Archive

THE PYLONS, 1935

In 1935, two 45-foot towers were constructed on either side of the stage. They were designed to house light and sound equipment, and engineered to minimize shadows and maximize sound.

The light board, then known as the "switchboard," was housed in the stage left structure, and the amplifying system was housed on stage right. Above, a bridge connected the twin pylons, and held the microphones and stage lights. The pylons were design by Gerhardt Kramer of the the architectural firm of Kramer & Harms.

Photo by Piaget Studio

PLANS FOR A MUNY FACELIFT, 1937

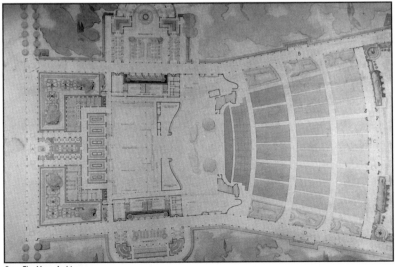

From The Muny Archive

The Muny conducted a city-wide architectural contest for the redesign of the "campus" in 1937. While the firm of Wischmeyer-Murphy won, the plan was not executed all at once, but rather in stages. Many of the improvements did not happen until after World War II, and some of the suggestions did not happen at all.

THE LEONARD CEELEY PIANO

Throughout the 1930s, the George Steck piano was the official piano of The Muny, supplied by the Aeolian Company in St. Louis. At the end of the season, The Muny would hold a sale of those pianos, signed by the stars of that summer. In 1938, Maryann Eustice-Spangler's father purchased one of those pianos for his twin daughters, autographed by Muny star Leonard Ceeley. Below are a few exerpts from a letter Maryann sent The Muny.

"When she [Maryann's piano teacher] told my parents that this baby grand was available, they instantly purchased it. It was offered at a slightly reduced price because it had been played once.

"What to do when both twins married? One twin didn't want the baby grand, and the other did. And so in 1946, I became the sole owner of this grand birthday gift!"

Maryann Spangler

From the 1934 Muny program.

THE EUSTICE TWINS

LEFT: Maryann
and
RIGHT:
Marjorie Eustice

Photos from the James Rausch Collection

THE PIANO

In 2015, Maryann generously donated her piano to The Muny.

ABOUT LEONARD CEELEY

British-born Leonard Ceeley was a frequent performer in St. Louis between 1930 and 1943. Often playing the swashbuckler or "heavy" roles, he starred at The Muny a total of 37 times. He was featured in the Marx brother's film *A Day At The Races* as a shady racetrack denizen. Ceeley performed on Broadway between 1924 and 1955, and his last performance in *The Boy Friend* supported Julie Andrews in her American stage debut.

LEFT: Leonard Ceeley as Pablo in *Nina Rosa*, 1931

Photo by Ruth Cunliff Russell

RICHARD (RED) SKELTON, 1938

Richard "Red" Skelton made his Muny debut in 1938, in *Gentlemen Unafraid*. That show was written by Oscar Hammerstein II and Jerome Kern, and co-produced by Broadway impressario Max Gordon. The Muny's production manager, Richard Berger, was rooting for Skelton to play the role, while Max Gordon was holding out for a young dancer from Belleville. Skelton, of course, won the part and actor Buddy Ebsen never did play The Muny. After a long and very successful career as a TV and radio comdedian, Skelton returned to The Muny in *The Red Skelton Show* in 1970 and '84.

LEFT: Richard "Red" Skelton's payroll card, 1938

RIGHT: The Muny's 1938 production of *Gentlemen Unafraid*. Red Skelton with Vicki Cummings

Photo by Ruth Cunliff Russell

PERMANENT PERGOLAS, 1938 - '39

From The Muny Archive

ABOVE: The old Muny facade with the wooden pergolas across the front.

RIGHT: The front pergolas as they are today.

While The Muny's covered walkways, also known as "pergolas," have changed their look through the years, their purpose has always been to shield a full Muny audience in case of rain. The concrete pergolas behind the free seats were installed in 1920-21. The wooden pergolas pictured at LEFT were constructed around that same time, and were replaced by the contemporary concrete pillars and roof in 1938-39.

Photo by Jerry Naunheim

THE GREATEST HITS OF THE 1930S

Photo by Ruth Cunliff Russell

RIO RITA, 1931

Set designs took on a new sophistication under the direction of the Shubert family.

KID BOOTS, 1936

Musicals like *Kid Boots* brought light-hearted diversions to Muny audiences still struggling in the Depression.

Photo by Ruth Cunliff Russell

Photo by Ruth Cunliff Russell

BABES IN TOYLAND, 1937

In the tradition of extravagant musicals created just for young people, The Muny"s 1937 production of *Babes in Toyland* didn't skimp on the size of the sets, nor the size of the cast.

AMERICA IN THE 1940S

- Average life expectancy for men was 60.8 years.
- Average cost of a gallon of gas was 11 cents.
- Average cost for a loaf of bread was 10 cents.
- Average cost for a new home was $3,920.
- Average cost of a new car was $850.
- Average annual wage was $1,725.
- Mt. Rushmore was completed.
- Only 55% of households had indoor plumbing.
- The cartoon characters of Tom and Jerry were created, and Disney's *Pinocchio* hit the silver screen.
- McDonald's opened their first restaurant in San Bernardino, California.
- Rice Krispies adopted the phrase "Snap! Crackle! Pop!"
- Velcro was invented.
- Jackie Robinson became the first African American to break the color barrier in Major League Baseball.
- The first Gold Record, indicating a sale of more than one million copies, was earned by Glenn Miller's "Chattanooga Choo-Choo."
- The bikini made its first appearance on American beaches.

STATE OF THE MUNY

"Throughout World War II, the Municipal Opera continued its summer series, despite almost insurmountable difficulties, because it was felt that the public needed gay and exhilarating entertainment more than ever in those depressing years. It was quite a problem to obtain leading men and male dancers, material for scenery was hard to get, and overcrowded transportation facilities and gasoline rationing prevented persons from traveling far. During that period, 1,000 seats were set aside nightly for servicemen and many other things were done to help the war effort."

FROM
ST. LOUIS' FABULOUS
OUTDDOOR THEATRE
BY CHARLES V. CLIFFORD

Throughout the early 1940s, Muny programs featured ads that reflected the first thing on everyone's mind: the War.

Repertory, 1940s

1940

The American Way	(June 3 - 16)
Naughty Marietta	(June 17 - 23)
Apple Blossoms	(June 24 - 30)
Rio Rita	(July 1 - 7)
The Chocolate Soldier	(July 8 - 14)
Good News	(July 15 - 21)
Knickerbocker Holiday	(July 22 - 28)
Anything Goes	(July 29 - August 4)
East Wind	(August 5 - 11)
Rosalie	(August 12 - 18)
Babes in Arms	(August 19 - 25)
The Great Waltz	(August 26 - September 1)

1941

New Orleans	(June 5 - 15)
Sweethearts	(June 16 - 22)
Too Many Girls	(June 23 - 29)
The Firefly	(June 30 - July 6)
The Three Musketeers	(July 7 - 13)
Irene	(July 14 - 20)
Nina Rosa	(July 21 - 27)
The Merry Widow	(July 28 - August 3)
Bitter Sweet	(August 4 - 10)
The Desert Song	(August 11 - 17)
The Red Mill	(August 18 - 24)
Balalaika	(August 25 - 31)

1942

Glamorous Night	(June 4 - 14)
Sally	(June 15 - 21)
The Song of the Flame	(June 22 - 28)
Hit the Deck	(June 29 - July 5)
No, No, Nanette	(July 6 - 12)
The New Moon	(July 13 - 19)
Girl Crazy	(July 20 - 26)
Wildflower	(July 27 - August 2)
Roberta	(August 3 – 9)
The Wizard of Oz	(August 10 - 16)
Show Boat	(August 17 - 30)

1943

Balalaika	(June 3 - 13)
Sunny	(June 14 - 20)
Rose Marie	(June 21 - 27)
Sons O' Guns	(June 28 - 4)
The Chocolate Soldier	(July 5 - 11)
The Great Waltz	(July 12 - 18)
Rosalie	(July 19 - 25)
The Desert Song	(July 26 - August 1)
Babes in Toyland	(August 2 - 8)
The Merry Widow	(August 9 - 15)
Chu Chin Chow	(August 16 - 29)

1944

The Open Road	(June 1 - 11)
Good News	(June 12 - 18)
The Vagabond King	(June 19 - 25)
Eileen	(June 25 - July 2)
Hit the Deck	(July 3 - 9)
Naughty Marietta	(July 10 - 16)
Music in the Air	(July 17 - 23)
Maytime	(July 24 - 30)
Irene	(July 31 - July 6)
The Bohemian Girl	(August 7 - 13)
The Red Mill	(August 14 - 20)
Rio Rita	(August 21 - 27)

1945

Jubilee	(June 7 - 17)
The O'Brien Girl	(June 18 - 24)
The Fortune Teller	(June 25 - July 1)
The New Moon	(July 2 - 8)
The Cat and the Fiddle	(July 9 - 15)
Madame Pompadour	(July 16 - 22)
The Firefly	(July 23 - 29)
The Pink Lady	(July 30 - August 5)
The Three Musketeers	(August 6 - 12)
Bitter Sweet	(August 13 - 19)
Sari	(August 20 - 26)
Roberta	(August 27 - September 2)

REPERTORY, 1940S

1946

The Desert Song	(June 6 - 16)
Mary	(June 17 - 23)
Gypsy Love	(June 24 - 30)
Rosalie	(July 1 - 7)
The Merry Widow	(July 8 - 14)
The Lost Waltz	(July 15 - 21)
East Wind	(July 22 - 28)
The Prince of Pilsen	(July 29 - August 4)
Robin Hood	(August 5 - 11)
The Wizard of Oz	(August 12 - 18)
The Great Waltz	(August 19 - September 1)

1947

The Dancing Years	(June 5 - 15)
Nina Rosa	(June 16 - 22)
No, No, Nanette	(June 23 - 29)
Rose Marie	(June 30 - July 6)
Apple Blossoms	(July 7 - 13)
Die Fledermaus	(July 14 - 20)
Sally	(July 21 - 27)
The Chimes of Normandy	(July 28 - August 3)
Naughty Marietta	(August 4 - 10)
Babes in Toyland	(August 11 - 17)
Show Boat	(August 18 - 31)

1948

Auld Lang Syne	(June 3 - 13)
Venus in Silk	(June 14 - 20)
Rio Rita	(June 21 - 27)
Hit the Deck	(June 28 - July 4)
The Three Musketeers	(July 5 - 11)
White Eagle	(July 12 - 18)
Jubilee	(July 19 - 25)
A Connecticut Yankee	(July 26 - August 1)
Sunny	(August 2 - 8)
Sari	(August 9 - 15)
Up in Central Park	(August 16 - 29)

1949

The New Moon	(June 9 - 19)
Bloomer Girl	(June 20 - 26)
The Fortune Teller	(June 27 - 3)
The Firefly	(July 4 - 10)
The Chocolate Soldier	(July 11 - 17)
Bitter Sweet	(July 18 - 24)
Irene	(July 25 - 31)
The Vagabond King	(August 1 - 7)
Roberta	(August 8 - 14)
The Red Mill	(August 15 - 21)
Song of Norway	(August 22 - September 5)

USHERING YOU IN

Photo courtesy of the Walsh Family

The photo at LEFT is a rare image of The Muny's 1944 usher staff. We can only guess how warm those formal uniforms must have been! The usher circled is James Walsh, whose family supplied the photo.

VINCENT PRICE
THE AMERICAN WAY, 1940

Vincent Price was already a name on Broadway and in Hollywood when he returned to his hometown to star in The Muny's production of *The American Way*. That show had run for 80 performances in New York before its St. Louis debut. Mr. Price returned to The Muny two more times, in 1976 as Fagin in *Oliver!*, and again in 1978 as the devilish Applegate in *Damn Yankees*. Mr. Price is remembered for his string of horror films, and was featured in *Edward Scissorhands* and Michael Jackson's *Thriller*.

RIGHT: A note from Mr. Price, sharing his "Muny Memories." Price states, "I have always treasured the many joys of being a St. Louisan and a player at The Muny."

BELOW: A photo of Price as Martin Gunther, in *The American Way*.

Photo by Ruth Cunliff Russell

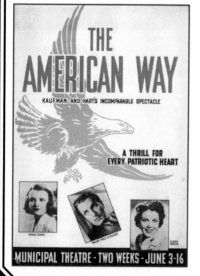

RIGHT:
Price's payroll record

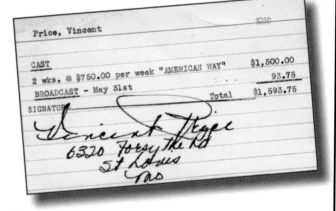

LEFT: A flier promoting *The American Way*.

THE MUNY GOES TO WAR

On December 8, 1941, the United States officially entered war with Japan, and when Germany declared war on America on December 11 of the same year, we were officially engaged in the global conflict. St. Louis – and consequently The Muny – were greatly affected, and this was clearly reflected in the programming, the content of our playbills, and in our concerted efforts to support the war effort.

AIR RAID WARNING

The Office of Civilian Defense has devised a plan to be used in the event of an air raid warning, which will place the audience under the protection of the reinforced concrete pergolas.

A careful check for years back shows 10 minutes to be the average time to clear the auditorium after the close of a performance. We have assurance from the authorities that there will be at least 30 minutes of warning before a hostile plane can pass over the city.

If such a warning should be received, definite orders will be given through the loud speaker system, which if followed under the direction of the ushers and police, will place the entire audience under this protection without undue crowding or inconvenience.

Obey instructions of those in charge

No automobiles will be allowed to move during a blackout.

ABOVE: Instructions to the audience in case of an air raid.

BELOW: An impressive scene from the 1943 production of *Sons O'Guns*. The military men were "recruited" from Jefferson Barracks.

From The Muny Archive

THE PASSING OF HENRY W. KIEL
NOVEMBER 26, 1942

Photo from the St. Louis Post-Dispatch

Henry Kiel, long-time mayor of St. Louis, played a crucial role in the establishment of The Muny. He supported the fledgling enterprise politically and financially, and convinced a cadre of influential St. Louisans to do the same. When the out-of-door theatre showed a loss during its first season, he famously went to downtown business owners and convinced them to purchase blocks of tickets for their friends, families and employees. Henry Kiel passed away on November 26, 1942. The Muny installed a plaque in the box office rotunda in honor of Kiel's priceless contributions

LEFT: Gaetano Cecere, instructor in sculpture at Washington University, poses with the design for a memorial plaque to honor Mayor Kiel. It was subsequently cut from Italian marble, and is still displayed in The Muny's box office area.

THE 25TH ANNIVERSARY, 1943

In 1943, with the country on the brink of World War II, The Muny celebrated its 25th summer in Forest Park. A gala season was produced, replete with lavish musicals, an array of favorite Muny performers, and accolades from the theatre community. The souvenir program pictured at right told the history of the theatre, and took a look forward into the unseeable future.

"You Have Done Much for Light Opera"

"I congratulate not only you and your personnel, and those who have made such a glorious success of the St. Louis Municipal Theatre, but also the fortunate residents of the city and its environs, who, for a quarter of a century, have made up your happy audiences.

"You . . . have done much for them and for light opera in America. The makers of American music should be, and are, proud of you."

JEROME KERN
The Composer

"Joy Afforded Tremendous Numbers"

"The joy afforded tremendous numbers of people before the war and the comfort given them during it should be a source of well-deserved gratification to you. . . . Let me hope that your work will continue for many successful years to come."

RICHARD RODGERS
The Composer

Images from The Muny's Silver Anniversary Program, 1943

Municpal Opera raises $35,000 for War, $9,600 for Army and Navy Relief Funds

Photo from the St. Louis Post-Dispatch

LEFT: War Stamp corsages were sold in the audience by members of the American Women's Voluntary Services, with the assistance of the Muny chorus. From left: Miss Katherine Salkey of the WVS, audience member Miss Catherine Bazdarich, and Miss Margaret Stinson, of the Muny chorus.

ABOVE: Even bread was sold with an eye to one's patriotic duties.

RIGHT: In 1942, the Women's Ensemble did their bit to entertain the troops with a backstage tour and photo op.

Photo by Ruth Cunliff Russell, from the collection of Mary Ann Hickey-Brickey. Ms. Brickey is on the far LEFT of the front row.

AFTER THE WAR

Municipal Opera Music Entertains Foreign Countries

Through the medium of radio, the thrilling music of Municipal Opera is being carried to many foreign countries this summer. For the fifth consecutive year, stars who appear in Municipal Opera productions and musical selections from repertories of the current and past seasons are being heard in a series of weekly half-hour programs on the nationwide network of the Columbia Broadcasting System. Originating in the studios of station KMOX, the programs are aired at 6 p. m. each Saturday.

In addition to the national hookup this year, the Municipal Opera programs are being shortwaved to Latin America in Spanish and Portuguese languages and to Europe during English and French language transmissions. Although the Municipal Opera programs were shortwaved to American armed forces overseas during the war, this is the first year they are being heard by foreign listeners.

Each program in the series includes narration on the guest soloists, selections, the following week's presentation and the traditions of St. Louis' Municipal Opera. Guest artists, who will play leading roles in the next week's Municipal Opera production, will be supported by a mixed chorus of 16 members of the Municipal Opera singing chorus. Familiar music from favorite operettas will be presented by an orchestra under the baton of Edwin McArthur, Municipal Opera musical director.

Visitors from out of town who have enjoyed the spectacle that is Municipal Opera will want to thrill again to the memory of music under the stars in the Forest Park theatre by listening to the Municipal Opera programs.

ABOVE LEFT: An ad from a 1949 Muny program urged readers to take good care of their cars. War shortages were not expected to fully ease for another two years.

ABOVE RIGHT: The Muny had broadcast versions of their musicals to the troops during the war. In tandem with KMOX radio, the program was expanded to both local and interntional hook-ups.

RIGHT: KSD-TV (later KSDK) advertised in The Muny's 1947 program. Television was to prove a new challenge in the years ahead.

WATSON BARRATT

MUNY SET DESIGNER AND ARTISTIC DIRECTOR

Prolific Broadway scenic designer Watson Barratt was brought to The Muny by the Shuberts in 1932, and designed there through 1934. He then took a Muny hiatus until 1941. From that year through 1943, he was the scenic designer and in 1943 added "art director and associate productions manager" to his title. When Barratt retired from The Muny in 1951, the story ran on the front page of the Globe-Democrat, above the fold. He is credited with the scenic design of more than 600 Broadway productions.

He designed the playbill cover pictured BELOW RIGHT, which was used from 1947 through 1951.

From The Muny Archive

Editor's Note: *The cover of this program was designed by Watson Barratt, Municipal Opera's Assistant Productions Manager and Art Director. Mr. Barratt's own description follows:*

"The Municipal Opera wouldn't be the same without the two famous oak trees—they practically spell 'Municipal Opera'—therefore it naturally gave me the motif for the new program design.

"A cover should be conceived from the standpoint of a decoration and not an illustration. For this reason I did not try to reproduce the stage of the Municipal Opera but used the oak leaves which represent our two trees and then seen through them is a glimpse of a tableau such as can be done on this stage as nowhere else in the country.

"I chose colors that were not realistic for that also not only makes it more effective as a decoration but precludes any possibility of it looking, as I said before, like an illustration."

The story below was written by Ron Elz, alias Johnny Rabbitt. Mr. Rabbitt is a local radio veteran, and a well-known St. Louis personality.

LEFT: An aerial view of the parking lot adjoining The Muny, on Easter Sunday, 1946.

Photo by Lloyd Spainhower, of the St. Louis Post-Dispatch

"Easter sunrise services were once enormous, non-denominational programs under the auspices of the Metropolitan Church Federation. They were initiated in 1926, and though ceremonies were actually held at sunrise, thousands would attend. A case in point is the service of April 2, 1935, when the sun rose at 5:16 a.m. to Mendelsohn's 'Sleepers, Wake' trumpet call. Attendance remained massive through WWII and a little beyond, but soon changing morés, population shifts and even drive-in movie theatres contributed to a dramatic decline. Non-denominational Easter Services are still held in Forest Park, although not at The Muny.

"In 1947, the first Easter Car Show took place on the upper Muny parking lot, and now that event has become a Muny-related tradition."

Ron Elz

MUNY FACE-LIFT, 1948

Post World War II, The Muny embarked on a physical improvement campaign that included adding seats to a section of the theatre that had been "lawn seating," and upgrading the chorus' dressing rooms.

NEW SEATING IN THEATRE

From The Muny Archive

CHORUS DRESSING ROOMS

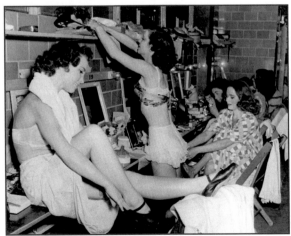

From The St. Louis Post-Dispatch

GREATEST HITS OF THE 1940S

Photo by Ruth Cunliff Russell

HIT THE DECK, 1942

The large guns in this photo were built to the scale of those found on a real battleship, and were constructed with the help of the local recruiting office.

BABES IN TOYLAND, 1943

Even the children's show took on a military aspect when the "kiddy chorus" joined the adult ensembles in *Babes In Toyland*.

Photo by Ruth Cunliff Russell

Photo by Ruth Cunliff Russell

ROBERTA, 1949

This elegant set was designed by Watson Barratt, and he considered this one of his most audience-pleasing designs. The fan was 40 feet at the base and 22 feet high. Members of the Ladies' Ensemble were the living decorations.

AMERICA in the 1950s

- Average life expectancy for men was 65.6 years.
- Average cost of a gallon of gas was 18 cents.
- Average cost for a loaf of bread was 12 cents.
- Average cost for a new home was $8,450.
- Average cost of a new car was $1,510.
- Average wage was $3,210.
- The polio vaccine, developed by Dr. Jonas Salk, was proven effective.
- Disneyland opened in 1955.
- The Bank of America issued the first credit card.
- M&M introduced its new slogan: "Melts in your mouth, not in your hand."
- In Montgomery, Alabama, Rosa Parks refused to give up her seat to a white person, initiating the bus boycott of 1955.
- The Barbie doll was first manufactured.
- The top 5 TV shows of 1950 were: *Texaco Star Theatre, Fireside Theatre, The Philco Television Playhouse, Your Show of Shows* and The *Colgate Comedy Hour*.

STATE OF THE MUNY

"In the early days of Muny Opera – the first decade – the repertory went in heavily for such things as *The Bohemian Girl, Robin Hood, Fra Diavolo* and *The Mikado*, and the audiences were composed largely of people 30 years and older. A conscious effort was then made to attract youth by using the works of such composers as Victor Herbert and Sigmund Romberg. It was successful. Today, it is sought to have a balanced repertory of old and new types of musical shows.

"Perhaps the turning point in Muny Opera's history came when we dropped the emphasis on attendance as a matter of civic duty, and went out for sheer superior showmanship."

St. Louis Post-Dispatch
Monday, July 10, 1950

THE DECADE OF RODGERS & HAMMERSTEIN

RIGHT: The week of August 14, 1950 was declared "Rodgers and Hammerstein Week," and St. Louisans were officially urged to attend.

"Sheer Showmanship," as noted in the official proclamation surely played a part in The Muny's resurgence in the post-war years. But there were two gentlemen, already friends of The Muny, who made the theatre in Forest Park a destination throughout the 1950s. They were Richard Rodgers and Oscar Hammerstein II, and the decade belonged to them.

A Banquet in Your Honor...

To kick off the 1950 Rodgers & Hammerstein Musical Festival, The Muny hosted a banquet in honor of the celebrated pair. Telegrams flew back and forth, a special themed menu was created, and details down to hand-designed place cards were put in place.

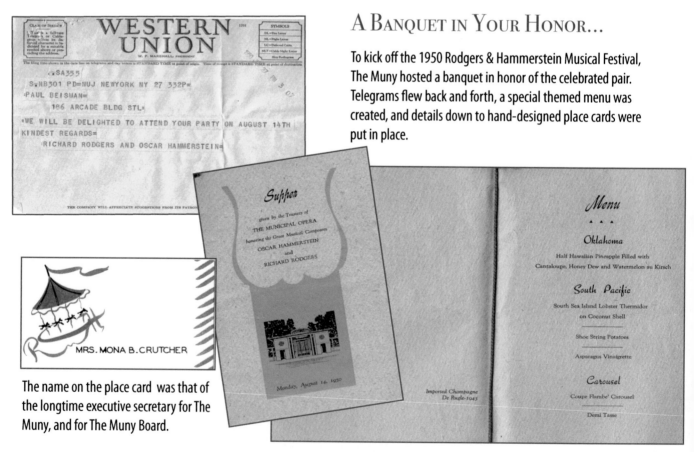

The name on the place card was that of the longtime executive secretary for The Muny, and for The Muny Board.

All artifacts from The Muny Archive

Repertory

1950s

1950

Brigadoon	(June 8 - 18)
Rosalie	(June 19 - 25)
East Wind	(June 26 - July 2)
Of Thee I Sing	(July 3 - 9)
Robin Hood	(July 10 - 16)
Lady in the Dark	(July 17 - 23)
The Desert Song	(July 24 - 30)
The Pink Lady	(July 31 - August 6)
Whoopee	(August 7 - 13)
Rodgers and Hammerstein Musical Festival	(August 14 - 20)
Carousel	(August 21 - Sept. 3)

1951

Nina Rosa	(June 7 - 17)
High Button Shoes	(June 18 - 24)
Music in the Air	(June 25 - July 1)
Miss Liberty	(July 2 - 8)
Die Fledermaus	(July 9 - 15)
Girl Crazy	(July 16 - 22)
Rodgers and Hammerstein Musical Festival	(July 23 - 29)
The Bohemian Girl	(July 30 - August 5)
The Merry Widow	(August 6 - 12)
The Wizard of Oz	(August 13 - 19)
The Great Waltz	(August 20 - Sept. 2)

1952

Show Boat	(June 5 - 15)
Sally	(June 16 - 22)
The Cat and the Fiddle	(June 23 - 29)
Rose Marie	(June 30 - July 6)
The Student Prince	(July 7 - 13)
The Bartered Bride	(July 14 - 20)
Countess Maritza	(July 21 - 27)
Mlle. Modiste	(July 28 - August 3)
Naughty Marietta	(August 4 - 10)
Babes in Toyland	(August 11 - 17)
Annie Get Your Gun	(August 18 - 31)

1953

Up in Central Park	(June 4 - 14)
Bloomer Girl	(June 15 - 21)
Cyrano de Bergerac	(June 22 - 28)
Rio Rita	(June 29 - July 5)
Blossom Time	(July 6 - 12)
Rip Van Winkle	(July 13 - 19)
No, No, Nanette	(July 20 - 26)
Carmen	(July 27 - August 2)
One Touch of Venus	(August 3 - 9)
Bitter Sweet	(August 10 - 16)
Kiss Me, Kate	(August 17 - 30)

1954

Call Me Madam	(June 3 - 13)
The New Moon	(June 14 - 20)
Song of Norway	(June 21 - 27)
Roberta	(June 28 - July 4)
The Mikado	(July 5 - 11)
Gentlemen Prefer Blondes	(July 12 - 18)
The Three Musketeers	(July 19 - 25)
Panama Hattie	(July 26 - August 1)
Where's Charley?	(August 2 - 8)
The Red Mill	(August 9 - 15)
Oklahoma!	(August 16 - 29)

1955

The Merry Widow	(June 2 - 12)
Brigadoon	(June 13 - 19)
Wonderful Town	(June 20 - 26)
The Vagabond King	(June 27 - July 3)
Guys and Dolls	(July 4 - 10)
The Desert Song	(July 11 - 17)
Rodgers & Hammerstein Concert	(July 18 - July 24)
Carousel	(July 25 - July 31)
Allegro	(August 1 - 7)
The King and I	(August 8 - 14)
South Pacific	(August 15 - 28)

REPERTORY
1950S

1956

Annie Get Your Gun	(June 7 - 17)
Paint Your Wagon	(June 18 - 24)
The Student Prince	(June 25 - July 1)
Hit the Deck	(July 2 - 8)
The Great Waltz	(July 9 - 15)
The Chocolate Soldier	(July 16 - 22)
Wish You Were Here	(July 23 - 29)
Kiss Me, Kate	(July 30 - August 5)
An Evening of Great Music	(August 6 - 12)
Peter Pan	(August 13 - 19)
Kismet	(August 20 - Sept. 2)

1957

South Pacific	(June 6 -16)
Plain and Fancy	(June 17 - 23)
Damn Yankees	(June 24 - 30)
The New Moon	(July 1 - 7)
Guys and Dolls	(July 8 -14)
Irene	(July 15 - 21)
Naughty Marietta	(July 22 - 28)
Can-Can	(July 29 - August 4)
An Evening of Great Music	(August 5 -11)
The Wizard of Oz	(August 12 - 18)
The Pajama Game	(August 18 - Sept. 1)

1958

Show Boat	(June 5 - 15)
Roberta	(June 16 - 22)
Silk Stockings	(June 23 - 29)
Rose Marie	(June 30 - July 6)
Lady in the Dark	(July 7 - 13)
On the Town	(July 14 - 20)
Rosalinda	(July 21 - 27)
Happy Hunting	(July 28 - August 3)
Finian's Rainbow	(August 4 - 10)
Hansel and Gretel/	
Act II, "The Nutcracker" Ballet	(August 11 - 17)
Oklahoma!	(August 18 - 31)

1959

The King and I	(June 11 - 21)
Song of Norway	(June 22 - 28)
Oh Captain	(June 29 - July 5)
Rio Rita	(July 6 - 12)
Gentlemen Prefer Blondes	(July 13 - 19)
Fanny	(July 20 - 26)
Li'l Abner	(July 27 - August 2)
Carmen	(August 3 - 9)
Call Me Madam	(August 10 - 16)
Babes in Toyland	(August 17 - 23)
Bells Are Ringing	(August 24 - Sept. 6)

After World War II came the Cold War, and Muny-goers were instructed as to the steps they should take in the event of a nuclear attack.

RODGERS & HAMMERSTEIN,
LYRICIST AND COMPOSER

From The Muny Archive

Richard Rodgers and Oscar Hammerstein II each had remarkable careers before they teamed up to form what is arguably the most successful Broadway song-writing team of all time.

Before their first collaborative production aired at The Muny, Richard Rodgers had written the music for five Muny musicals, including *A Connecticut Yankee, On Your Toes, Babes in Arms, The Boys from Syracuse* and *Pal Joey*. Oscar Hammerstein had written the lyrics and often the book for 14 musicals, including *Rose Marie, The Desert Song,* and the perennial classic, *Show Boat*.

When Rodgers & Hammerstein began working together, the result was pure musical magic. Their masterworks include *South Pacific, Oklahoma!, Carousel, The King and I* and *The Sound of Music*.

Both Rodgers and Hammerstein had a special relationship with The Muny. ABOVE, Oscar Hammerstein is pictured in the Muny auditorium, overseeing the 1938 production of *Gentlemen Unafraid*. Richard Rodgers (RIGHT) in The Muny audience with his wife, Dorothy, for the world stage premiere of *State Fair* (1969).

Souvenir Programs from The Muny Archive

From The Muny Archive

IN THE AUDIENCE

Important and interesting people seemed to just pop into The Muny to catch a world class musical throughout the 1950s. A few of them are pictured below.

AN AUDIENCE WITH GLORIA SWANSON, 1950

From The Muny Archive

Screen Queen Gloria Swanson (SECOND FROM RIGHT) enjoyed a Muny performance as the guest of then-St. Louis Mayor Darst and his wife. Her daughter, also named Gloria Swanson (Somborn), is seated at the far LEFT.

"IN MY HUMBLE OPINION, THE ST. LOUIS MUNICIPAL THEATRE IS THE FINEST OUTDOOR THEATRE IN THE WORLD TODAY – ACOUSTICALLY, SCENICALLY, AND EVERY OTHER WAY." EDDIE CANTOR, 1952

Veteran comedian Eddie Cantor made a backstage visit on 1952's closing night of *Annie Get Your Gun*. With Mr. Cantor are Muny chorus girls Jeanne Reardon, Mary Jo Goodson, Sally Reichert and Barbara Allen.

Photo from the St. Louis Post-Dispatch

BACKSTAGE WITH EDDIE CANTOR 1952

"IF THIS FABULOUS THEATER EXISTED IN EUROPE, THE CABLE WIRES WOULD BE BRISTLING WITH STORIES OF ITS GREATNESS!" ED SULLIVAN, 1953

A REALLY BIG SHOW ED SULLIVAN, 1953

From The Muny Archive

Ed Sullivan, then host of *Toast of the Town,* made a visit to Forest Park to take in *Up in Central Park,* 1953.

THE YEAR OF RODGERS & HAMMERSTEIN

1955

1955 might well be called "The Year of Rodgers & Hammerstein." The season featured a six-week festival, opening with a *Rodgers and Hammerstein Concert* attended by both men, and with Rodgers conducting the overture. *Allegro, Carousel,* and *The King and I* each played a week, with *South Pacific* making its Muny debut and closing the summer with a two-week run.

CAROUSEL

Carousel first played The Muny in 1950 and was revived for the 1955 season. In the inaugural 1950 production, Virginia Haskins played the luckless Julie Jordan, and Jack Kilty her Billy Bigelow.

Photo by Ruth Cunliff Russell

THE KING AND I

The Muny's very first production of *The King and I* debuted in 1955. Mrs. Anna was played by Annamary Dickey and Terry Saunders was Lady Thiang. Ms. Saunders had played the role on Broadway (although she did not originate it), and repeated her performance in the 1956 film.

Photo by Ferman Photography

Photo by Ferman Photography

SOUTH PACIFIC

South Pacific had debuted in New York in 1949, but it didn't play The Muny until six years later. Former St. Louisan Richard Eastham played Emile DeBecque, and Kyle MacDonnell was Nellie Forbush.

Keeping Cool
1955

Two huge fans, like those used in citrus groves and airports to disperse fog, were added at the extreme sides of the theatre. This solution was suggested by Dr. A. Thomas, president of Monsanto Chemical Company.

The fans were made entirely of aluminum, and included a 9.5-foot propeller on top of a 30-foot tower.

ABOVE

Water was trickled down the concrete steps of the theatre during the hottest part of the day. The idea was this thin film of water would prevent heat from being absorbed by and stored up in the concrete. What it actually produced was steam.

ABOVE

In 1955, four big blowers were installed to draw in fresh air and circulate in the lower section of the auditorium. These could be left running during a performance as they were very quiet, but the dispersal fans could only be used before the show and at intermissions.

Muny Program ads from Emerson Electric detailing state-of-the-art home cooling. ABOVE, 1958   RIGHT, 1954

Bob Hope in ROBERTA, 1958

From The Muny Archive

In 1958, international comedy star and actor Bob Hope made a special appearance at The Muny, recreating the role of Huckleberry Haines in *Roberta*. His Broadway performance in that part is credited with bringing Hope to national attention. His daughter Linda played the part of Luella LaVerne, and she matriculated to St. Louis University shortly after. While in St. Louis, Mr. Hope made himself at home, golfing at the Old Warson Country Club and enjoying a party with Sam, the Watermelon Man. Missouri Senator Stuart Symington is credited for convincing Hope to appear here, and for first encouraging Mr. Hope to entertain the troops.

Photo and typed comments from Mickey McTague

LEFT: Bob Hope with Missouri Senator Stuart Symington.

RIGHT: Bob Hope with co-star Terry Saunders, in *Roberta.*

From The Muny Archive

St. Louis Post-Dispatch, June 9, 1958

LEFT: Linda Hope, Bob's daughter, relaxes with her father on The Muny's rehearsal platform during a break.

RIGHT: Bob Hope trades watermelon and quips with Sam, the Watermelon Man.

St. Louis Post-Dispatch, August 25, 1958

Photo by Ruth Cunliff Russell

BRIGADOON, 1950

Brigadoon marked the Muny debut of Alan Jay Lerner and Frederick Loewe musicals. If a duo of songwriters were to prove a challenge to the ascendancy of Rodgers and Hammerstein, it would be this pair.

CALL ME MADAM, 1954

Future Broadway diva Elaine Stritch, who had served as Ethel Merman's understudy in the Broadway production of *Call Me Madam*, played Sally Adams at The Muny. Here Miss Stritch, (second from the right) pauses near The Muny's dressing rooms with her co-stars.

Photo by Ruth Cunliff Russell

THE THREE MUSKETEERS, 1954

While Lerner & Loewe and Rodgers & Hammerstein were in the forefront of the new guard, the operetta was not completely forgotten. This marked the last production of *The Three Musketeers* The Muny would produce.

Photo by Ruth Cunliff Russell

AMERICA in the 1960s

- Average life expectancy for men was 66.6 years.
- Average cost of a gallon of gas was 25 cents.
- Average cost for a loaf of bread was 22 cents.
- Average cost for a new home was $12,700.
- Average cost of a new car was $2,600.
- Average wage was $5,315.
- The top TV shows of 1960 were: *Gunsmoke, Wagon Train, Have Gun - Will Travel* and *The Andy Griffith Show*.
- In 1962, Wal-Mart opened its first store.
- John F. Kennedy was America's youngest elected president in 1960. He was assassinated in 1963.
- The Ford Mustang, destined to become Ford's flagship muscle car, debuted in 1964.
- The Civil Rights Act was signed into law in 1964.
- In 1964, the Beatles made their ground-breaking appearance on the Ed Sullivan Show.
- The first Super Bowl was played in 1967.
- Cassius Clay changed his name to Muhammad Ali.
- In 1969, Neil Armstrong became the first human to walk on the moon.

Times Have Changed; So Has the Muny Opera
Romantic Operettas and River Des Peres Have Both Gone Under in Park—Modern Composers Now Call Tune

St. Louis Post-Dispatch, May 28, 1963

STATE OF THE MUNY

"Gentlemen, usually when I'm invited to join you at luncheon I bring you a report on productions details such as repertory and the casting of important stars. Today I feel compelled to speak in a different vein.

"Compared to the present, the theatre of the 1940s was uncomplicated — with no special problems — no night baseball, night racing, air-conditioning or television, only about five professional musical theatres and little or no competition from barn theatres. Actors sought us in a buyer's market. We were indeed, 'Alone In Our Greatness.'

"Contrast that period with the present and we have a very different picture. Now we have 44 Equity musical theatres and 116 dramatic theatres. In addition, locally, we have night baseball, night racing, and air-conditioning. We have a population that has exploded into the suburbs away from the Opera. However, the three most important and powerful influences are the birth of the Tent theatre, coast-to-coast television, and the entrance of the big talent agencies into our field."

John Kennedy
Manager, The Municipal Theatre
Addressing the Board of Directors Meeting
May 27, 1963

The 1960 Muny program cover at RIGHT proclaimed the illustration to be "theatre's proudest coat of arms." The line of music directly above the "Alone...In Its Greatness" banner are the opening notes of "Old Man River."

The Muny's 1962 program touted the eminent opening of the Planetarium.

A CRITIC REMEMBERS THE '60S

"My parents took me and my sister, Marcy, to The Muny every week. We grew up learning all the songs from all the shows – *My Fair Lady* and *Annie Get Your Gun, South Pacific* and *West Side Story, Bye Bye Birdie* and *Kiss Me, Kate,* on and on and on.

"Maybe more importantly, we learned the structure of classic musical theater: the difference between the leading couple and the second pair, the way some shows depended on sentiment and others on wit, the value of a great eleven o'clock number.

"Those turned out to be vital lessons, whether we were revisiting old favorites or seeing shows that experimented with long-established conventions to bring musical theater into a new era for a new century.

"Vital lessons? Let's be honest: They turned out to be job skills."

Judith Newmark

Theatre Critic,
St. Louis Post-Dispatch

A SISTER SNITCHES

"According to family lore, Judy issued her first theater critique before the age of four. It was her first time at The Muny - or any stage production. The name of the show has been lost to history, but we do know that before the performance ended, Judy requested that our parents change the channel!"

Marcy Cornfeld

Muny Archivist and
Judy's little sister.

From the personal collection of Marcy Cornfeld

The Jackoway sisters, Marcy (LEFT) and Judy, all dressed up for a night at The Muny.

REPERTORY
1960s

1960

Meet Me In St. Louis	(June 9 - 19)
Kismet	(June 20 - 26)
Anything Goes	(June 27 - July 3)
The Desert Song	(July 4 - 10)
The Student Prince	(July 11 - 17)
Tom Sawyer	(July 18 - 24)
Rosalie	(July 25 - 31)
Madame Butterfly	(August 1 - 7)
Knights of Song	(August 8 - 14)
The Red Mill	(August 15 - 21)
Redhead	(August 22 - Sept. 4)

1961

Calamity Jane	(June 12 - 25)
Take Me Along	(June 26 - July 2)
The Great Waltz	(July 3 - 9)
Kiss Me, Kate	(July 10 - 16)
Destry Rides Again	(July 17 - 23)
Robin Hood	(July 24 - 30)
Wish You Were Here	(July 31 - August 6)
Can-Can	(August 7 - 13)
Cinderella	(August 14 - 20)
Flower Drum Song	(August 21 - Sept. 3)

1962

Around the World in 80 Days	(June 11 - 24)
Molly Darling	(June 25 - July 1)
The Pajama Game	(July 2 - 8)
Mexican Holidays:	
Mexican Folklore Festival	(July 9 - 15)
Bye Bye Birdie	(July 16 - 22)
Annie Get Your Gun	(July 23 - 29)
Blossom Time	(July 30 - August 5)
Oklahoma!	(August 6 - 2)
The Wizard of Oz	(August 13 - 19)
The Music Man	(August 20 - Sept. 2)

1963

Carnival	(June 10 - 23)
I Dream of Jeanie	(June 24 - 30)
Li'l Abner	(July 1 - 7)
Brigadoon	(July 8 - 14)
The Unsinkable	
Molly Brown	(July 15 - 21)
Babes in Toyland	(July 22 - 28)
The King and I	(July 29 - August 4)
Gypsy	(August 5 - 11)
South Pacific	(August 12 - 8)
West Side Story	(August 19 - Sept. 1)

1964

My Fair Lady	(June 8 - 21)
Show Boat	(June 22 - 28)
Mr. President	(June 29 - July 5)
Carousel	(July 6 - 12)
Tom Sawyer	(July 13 - 19)
Milk and Honey	(July 20 - 26)
Damn Yankees	(July 27 - August 2)
The Boys from Syracuse	(August 3 - 9)
Porgy and Bess	(August 10 - 16)
The Sound of Music	(August 17 - Sept. 6)

1965

Meet Me In St. Louis	(June 7 - 20)
Guys and Dolls	(June 21 - 27)
Here's Love!	(June 28 - July 4)
110 in the Shade	(July 5 - 11)
Little Me	(July 12 - 18)
Cinderella	(July 19 - 25)
The Student Prince	(July 26 - August 1)
High Button Shoes	(Auust 2 - 8)
Flower Drum Song	(August 9 - 15)
Camelot	(August 16 - Sept. 5)

REPERTORY
1960s

1966

The Music Man	(June 6 - 19)
Good News	(June 20 - 26)
Kiss Me, Kate	(June 27 - July 3)
The Desert Song	(July 4 - 10)
Can-Can	(July 11 - 17)
Bye Bye Birdie	(July 18 - 24)
Oklahoma!	(July 25 - 31)
Bells Are Ringing	(August 1 - 7)
Hansel and Gretel/ Act II "The Nutcracker" Ballet	(August 8 - 14)
How to Succeed in Business Without Really Trying	(August 15 - 28)

1967

West Side Story	(June 5 - 18)
Wish You Were Here	(June 19 - 25)
Do I Hear A Waltz?	(June 26 - July 2)
Superman	(July 3 - 9)
The New Moon	(July 10 - 16)
The Unsinkable Molly Brown	(July 17 - 23)
Funny Girl	(July 24 - 30)
The Royal Ballet	(August 1 - 6)
On A Clear Day You Can See Forever	(August 7 - 13)
Gypsy	(August 14 - 20)
The King and I	(August 21 - Sept. 3)

1968

My Fair Lady	(June 3 - 16)
The Pajama Game	(June 17 - 23)
Annie Get Your Gun	(June 24 - 30)
The Merry Widow	(July 1 - 7)
Brigadoon	(July 8 - 14)
Carousel	(July 15 - 21)
Call Me Madam	(July 22 - 28)
Hello, Dolly!	(July 29 - August 3)
Show Boat	(August 5 - 11)
The Wizard of Oz	(August 12 - 18)
The Sound of Music	(August 19 - Sept. 1)

1969

State Fair	(June 2 - 15)
Kismet	(June 16 - 22)
Camelot	(June 23 - 29)
The Most Happy Fella	(June 30 - July 6)
Mame	(July 7 - 20)
The Royal Ballet	(July 21 - 27)
Damn Yankees	(July 28 - August 3)
Guys and Dolls	(August 4 - 10)
South Pacific	(August 11 - 17)
Snow White and the Seven Dwarfs	(August 18 - 31)

RALPH BLANE: COMPOSER AND MUNY CHORUS BOY

Composer Ralph Blane began life as Ralph Hunsecker. In 1934, 20-year-old Hunsecker performed in The Muny's "Gentlemen's Ensemble." In 1945, in collaboration with Hugh Martin, Blane penned the tunes "The Boy Next Door," "The Trolley Song" and "Have Yourself a Merry Little Christmas." *Meet Me In St. Louis* is his best known work.

From The Muny Archive

WORLD STAGE PREMIERE, 1960
MEET ME IN ST. LOUIS

Photo by Harold Ferman

LEFT: Author Sally Benson
ABOVE: An ad for The Muny's premiere production of *Meet Me In St. Louis.*

Sally Benson was a native St. Louisan, and the author of "The Kensington Stories," upon which *Meet Me In St. Louis* was based. She had confessed to being the "Tootie" in the story, and was in the Muny audience for its stage premiere in 1960. Joseph Laitin, a special correspondent of the Post-Dispatch, interviewed Ms. Benson in Hollywood just before the St. Louis premiere.

"When I sold it to MGM. for a movie, I retained the stage rights," Benson said, "but MGM wouldn't release the songs, so Ralph Blane and Hugh Martin wrote eight more songs. We're going to clean up with it this summer. 46 theatres all over the country have booked it. We'll make a mint."

RAISING THE BOOM
1961

The fact that the Muny stage does not have a ceiling has always been problematic, especially when it comes to hanging curtains. In order to make expedient set changes, a unique solution was found for a unique challenge. A movable steel framework, designed to carry painted canvases, was installed.

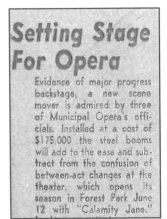

Setting Stage For Opera

Evidence of major progress backstage, a new scene mover is admired by three of Municipal Opera's officials. Installed at a cost of $175,000 the steel booms will add to the ease and subtract from the confusion of between-act changes at the theater, which opens its season in Forest Park June 12 with "Calamity Jane."

From the St. Louis Post-Dispatch

From The Muny Archive

ABOVE: What the booms look like when they are bare of a stage dressing.

Photo by Jim Herren

LEFT: How the booms look when they are "dressed," or covered by a painted canvas.

BETTY WHITE
1961, '63, '66

Betty White made three Muny appearances, the first as Lily in *Take Me Along* (1961), and the second as Mrs. Anna in *The King and I* (1963). Her most recent Muny role was that of Ella in *Bells Are Ringing* (1966), co-starring with her husband, Allen Ludden.

In the letter at RIGHT, Ms. White remembers her 1963 appearance as Mrs. Anna as a treasured memory, "because it was part of my honeymoon. Allen Ludden and I had just been married six weeks."

LEFT: In BELLS ARE RINGING, 1966.

Photos from The Muny Archive

PELAGIE GREEN, 1962

Pelagie Green was the first African-American to be chosen for The Muny's dancing ensemble in a "color blind" selection. Ms. Green was the pioneer in the practice of casting a person of color in a role that was not specifically written for that race. So in 1962, Ms. Green was a townsperson in *Tom Sawyer*, one of Esther's chums on the trolley in *Meet Me In St. Louis,* and an Iowa-stubborn townsperson in *The Music Man*. A dance instructor for many years, Ms. Green passed away in 2013.

Photos courtesy of the St. Louis Post-Dispatch.
Photo on right by Laurie Skrivan

Denny Reagan
1968

Photo by Phillip Hamer

From The Muny Archive

ABOVE: Denny Reagan, Muny President & CEO.
RIGHT: Denny Reagan, on the Muny clean-up team, C1968.

"'When I was 16, I just wanted a job and I had a friend who helped me get on the clean-up crew with him,' said Reagan. 'Honestly, it was just a summer job. My dad never took the family to shows. It just didn't happen.'

"What did happen, after he was hired, was a loyal commitment to the St. Louis Muny. Before being named president in 1991, he advanced from the clean-up team to wardrobe dresser, stage crew, runner, courier, office clerk, office manager, the manager of theater operations and assistant general manager.

"As president and CEO, he has overseen more than $25 million in Muny improvements, including larger seats, new concession and restroom amenities, and better fans to cool down audiences on hot summer evenings."

Don Corrigan
The Webster-Kirkwood Times
December, 2017

Changing of the Guard

Edwin McArthur

From The Muny Archive

John Kennedy

From The Muny Archive

The Muny Board made a decision at the end of the 1967 season not to renew the contracts of long time music director Edwin McArthur and artistic director John Kennedy.
Muny audiences protested, and even initiated a petition to retain McArthur, but the following year, Anton Coppola conducted. Glenn Jordan was named artistic director for the 1968 season.

Glenn Jordan

From The Muny Archive

RIGHT: Glenn Jordan was recruited from the St. Paul Civic Opera. He served as The Muny's production director from 1968 through 1970. Under his leadership, The Muny moved from a stock team of creatives – directors, choreographers, and designers – to a a system employing a different team for each show.

THE 50TH ANNIVERSARY SEASON
1968

CALL ME MADAM
ETHEL MERMAN & RUSSELL NYPE

From The Muny Archive

Ethel Merman recreated her Broadway triumph as Sally Adams for The Muny's 50th Anniversary Season in *Call Me Madam*.

> "THE THEATRE IS INDEED WONDERFUL, AND I HOPE THAT IT REACHES WHATEVER A DOUBLE GOLDEN ANNIVERSARY IS."
> RICHARD RODGERS

SHOW BOAT
ARTHUR GODFREY & MARY WICKES

From The Muny Archive

In 1968, radio icon Arthur Godfrey starred as Cap'n Andy with hometown girl Mary Wickes as his Parthy Ann Hawks. This would be Godfrey's only Muny appearance. Ms. Wickes was The Muny's favorite character actress for many years.

From The Muny Archive

HELLO, DOLLY!
PEARL BAILEY & CAB CALLOWAY

In an unprecedented move, the hit Broadway musical *Hello, Dolly!* starring
Pearl Bailey and Cab Calloway closed in New York to play The Muny. Both
Bailey and Calloway would return in 1971 for a repeat performance "by
popular demand." Mr. Calloway also starred as Sportin' Life in *Porgy and Bess*
(1964). "Pearlie May" brought her one woman show, *The Pearl Bailey Show*,
to The Muny for one night only in 1972.

ST. LOUIS
MUNICIPAL OPERA
50TH ANNIVERSARY WEEK
JULY 29-
AUGUST 3
1968

HELLO, DOLLY!

From The Muny Archive

MY FAIR LADY
DOUGLAS FAIRBANKS, JR. & EDDIE ALBERT

From The Muny Archive

Eddie Albert, star of the big and little screen, made two Muny
appearances in the 1960s. The first was as Harold Hill in *The Music Man*
(1966). He returned for The Muny's 50th anniversary season as Alfred P.
Doolittle in *My Fair Lady,* opposite Douglas Fairbanks, Jr. as Henry Higgins.
My Fair Lady is Fairbanks' only Muny performance.

THE SOUND OF MUSIC
FLORENCE HENDERSON

Florence Henderson made her Muny debut as Maria in *The Sound of Music* (1968). She
quickly became a Muny favorite, and returned an additional four times.

From The Muny Archive

Herb Alpert & The Tijuana Brass

HERB ALPERT & THE TIJUANA BRASS, 1968

"It was a great night for teenagers, but to some of the older generation, it
sounded very repetitious. Even Harper Barnes of the Post-Dispatch, while giving
a very glowing review, thought that a few of the pieces were played 'twice, or
maybe it just felt that way.' It could not be proved because there were no printed
programs."

Charles V. Clifford

Disney's First Stage Musical
Snow White, 1969

Disney Studio Officials Here For Snow White at Muny Opera

From the St. Louis Globe-Democrat

From The Muny Archive

In 1969, in one of its very first forays onto the stage, Disney's *Snow White and the Seven Dwarfs* made its Muny debut.

Walt Disney's brother, Roy, was on hand for the opening. Billy Barty starred as Dopey, and a repeat production played at The Muny in 1972.

From The Muny Archive

From The Muny Archive

ABOVE: Costume test for Patricia Wise as Snow White
RIGHT: Costume test for Marthe Erroll as the Queen

MAME
And The Man on The Moon, 1969

"On closing night of our *Mame* production, July 20, 1969, the audience roared with laughter during the number "The Man In The Moon Is A Lady." A couple of hours earlier a man may have literally made the discovery when astronaut Neil Armstrong set foot on the moon."

By BRAD HOLIDAY
Brad Holiday was a St. Louis performer, who appeared at The Muny 22 times between 1966 and 1991.

Dee Hoty as Mame (2005). Photo by Jim Herren

WOLRD PREMIERE: STATE FAIR, 1969

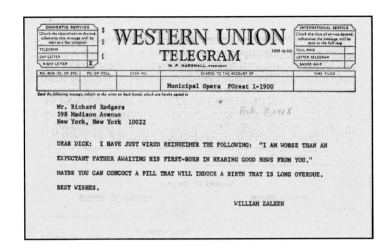

LEFT: In a telegram dated February 3, 1968, Muny manager William Zalken pleaded with composer Richard Rodgers for an answer. Judging by the date, it seems that Zalken hoped that the world stage premiere of *State Fair* would take place in 1968, our anniversary season. History tells us that the "birth" of which Zalken spoke did not take place until a year later.

BELOW: The title page for the world premiere of the stage version of *State Fair*. Then-unknown Tommy Tune served as choreographer, and also took the role of "Tommy." The musical director was Anton Coppola, uncle of film director Francis Ford Coppola.

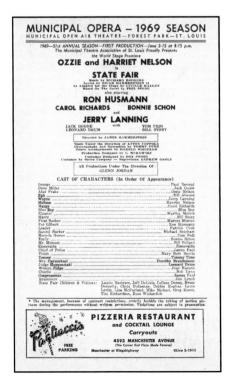

ABOVE: The St. Louis Post-Dispatch featured the stars of *State Fair* on the cover of its June 1, 1969 Pictures section. Ozzie and Harriet Nelson headlined the musical.

Greatest Hits of the 1960s

In the 1960s, The Muny ventured into producing several world premiere musicals. Three of them are illustrated below.

Photo by Ferman Photography

Molly Darling, 1962

Fran (lyrics) and Jay Landesmann (co-author, book), noted St. Louis Bohemians and authors of *The Nervous Set,* penned an original musical, *Molly Darling* for The Muny

Around The World in 80 Days, 1962

Cyril Ritchard starred in the world stage premiere of Michael Todd's *Around the World in 80 Days.*

Photo by Ferman Photography

Photo by Ferman Photography

I Dream of Jeanie, 1963

I Dream of Jeanie featured the music of Stephen Foster, and highlighted a rich and romantic life on the Mississippi in the days before the Civil War.

AMERICA in the 1970s

- Average life expectancy for men was 67.1 years.
- Average cost of a gallon of gas was 36 cents.
- Average cost for a loaf of bread was 25 cents.
- Average cost for a new home was $23,450.
- Average cost of a new car was $3,450.
- Average annual wage was $9,400.
- The top five TV shows of 1970 were: *Marcus Welby, M.D.; The Flip Wilson Show; Here's Lucy; Ironside* and *Gunsmoke*.
- In 1974, Richard Nixon became the only US President to ever resign from office.
- In 1971, Federal Express Corporation opened their door.
- In 1978, the first healthy "test-tube baby," Louise Brown, was born.

STATE OF THE MUNY

"The relative brevity and late start of the 1972 Municipal Opera season is, as much as anything, a reflection of changing times. The fact is that the family-type operettas and musical extravaganzas that were the staple fare of The Muny for so many years have been going out of fashion. It is increasingly difficult to obtain productions suitable for the big outdoor theater in Forest Park.

"William Zalken, manager of The Muny, touched on some of the probems in a recent interview with Myles Standish of our staff. He pointed out, for example, that many Broadway hit musicals such as *Hair* and *Oh! Calcutta!* are obviously unacceptable to Muny audiences, and the field upon which to draw is otherwise limited. Big stars demand big fees.

"It seems to us that in view of the times the Muny management as been imaginative and innovative – there are excellent attractions on the schedule this year – but there is no blinking the fact that the long-range future of the opera does not look as bright as it did, say, in the 1920s and 1930s. We feel confident new challenges will be met in the future as they have in the past, but it may take a little doing."

An Editorial
St. Louis Post-Dispatch
May 18, 1972

> "Municpal Opera shortened its coming season by three weeks and two shows, but the sale of season tickets at a price about the same or slightly higher than last season, was reported by the management as phenomenal, and likely to set a record."
>
> Myles Standish,
> St. Louis Post-Dispatch

Myles Standish
Bad Stage Season Financially Here

LIVE PROFESSIONAL THEATER has taken a financial drubbing in the St. Louis area during the season just closed. The American Theater, stalwart of the "legit" in St. Louis for 53 years, had only six shows running 14 weeks. The gross was dismal, only somewhere around $300,000. It was the lowest since the 1959-1960 season when the theater had its last year at its former Grand boulevard location, when the figure was $254,000.

The gross for the past season was less than a third of recent seasons. For instance, the 1961-62 season grossed $940,000, the 1957-68 season $1,031,500, and the following season slightly less. Last season's number of productions and weeks played dipped below the 12 productions in 15½ weeks of 1956-59 and was the lowest since the days of the Depression.

The city's only stock company, that run by producer Jean Webster Tsokos at the Sir John Falstaff Theater in the Spanish Pavilion, was closed last Sunday as a result of the foreclosure on and closing of the Pavilion by its mortgage holder. That the operator, the United Theater Company, which opened the theater nine months ago with a system of guest stars and a stock company, was having its own financial troubles was indicated by the fact that a lien for $35,410 for delinquent withholding and social security taxes for the three months ending Dec. 31 was filed against it by the federal collector of internal revenue. Attendance had generally been poor. Mrs. Tsokos could not be reached for a statement, but she had said it would take at least two months to reopen the theater, if and when the Pavilion is reopened.

THE AREA'S REGIONAL theater, the Loretto-Hilton Center at Webster College, which had had a brilliant season with a resident company and guest stars, canceled its last play in March, a world premiere two-week run of "Bedford Forrest," because of money troubles. Walter Perner, the managing director, said the company was $200,000 in the red for the season, as it had been the two previous seasons. The theater had been subsidized by the college during the four years of its existence to the tune of about $700,000. Perner said at the time the finances would be reorganized, and he expected to reopen the center again in the fall provided a drive for funds by the college itself were successful. There was a hopeful situation in that the theater's gross had more than doubled that of the previous year, and was expected to increase still more in future seasons.

Municipal Opera shortened its coming season by three weeks and two shows, but the sale of season tickets at a price about the same or slightly higher than last season, was reported by the management as phenomenal and likely to set a record. So the argument that was the country hovering on the brink of a recession the first thing hit in show business is the live theater, wouldn't apply here.

St. Louis Post-Dispatch, April 26, 1970

Robert Goulet, Prom Magazine and The Muny by Ron Elz

"For decades, Prom magazine and The Muny were, at least for high school kids, inextricably linked. This was due to a special arrangement in which Julian Miller, founder and publisher of Prom, would get free tickets to opening night of Muny productions that he would personally award to select students from all area high schools. The lucky recipients who often got their first taste of professional musical theatre with their gratis ticket were usually Prom reporters. These 'reporters' (of which there were 2 for each school) were chosen by Miller, and their 'term' was for one semester.

"While Muny managers such as today's gregarious Denny Reagan officially greeted theatre guests inside, Julian greeted his guests under the pergola just outside of the ticket windows. Prom was published from 1947 to 1973. The mists of time have erased just when this Muny tradition began and ended. Prom has been gone for 45 years, Julian passed away in 2001 at the age of 85, and today Prom magazines are sought-after collectibles."

Ron Elz

Robert Goulet held a meet-and-greet with Prom reporters in 1971. Goulet was in town for his one man/one night show.

Repertory, 1970s

1970

Promises, Promises	(July 6 - 12)
Oliver!	(July 13 - 9)
Man of La Mancha	(July 20 - 26)
Oklahoma!	(July 27 - August 2)
How to Succeed in Business Without Really Trying	(August 3 - 9)
George M!	(August 10 - 16)
Fiddler on the Roof	(August 17 - 30)
Moiseyev Dance Company	(Sept. 1 - 6)

1971

The Stuttgart Ballet	(June 14 - 20)
Hello, Dolly!	(June 28 - July 3)
Applause	(July 5 - 11)
Sweet Charity	(July 19 - 25)
The Music Man	(July 26 - August 1)
Two by Two	(August 2 - 8)
The Unsinkable Molly Brown	(August 9 - 15)
Cabaret	(August 16 - 22)
The King and I	(August 23 - 29)
This is Show Business	(August 30 - Sept. 5)

1972

Follies	(July 3 - 9)
Ukrainian Dance Company	(July 18 - July 23)
1776	(July 24 - 30)
The Liza Minnelli Show	(July 31 - August 6)
Snow White and the Seven Dwarfs	(August 7 - 13)
Anything Goes	(August 14 - 20)
The Student Prince	(August 21 - 27)
The Sound of Music	(August 28 - Sept. 3)

1973

No, No, Nanette	(July 2 - 8)
South Pacific	(July 9 - 15)
Fiddler on the Roof	(July 16 - 22)
Seesaw	(July 23 - 29)
Lorelei	(July 30 - August 5)
Irene	(August 6 - 12)
The Bolshoi Ballet	(August 13 - 19)
Two Gentlemen of Verona	(August 20 - 26)
Gigi	(August 28 - Sept. 9)

1974

Take Me Along	(July 1 - 7)
Over Here!	(July 8 - 14)
I Do! I Do!	(July 15 - 21)
Man of La Mancha	(July 22 - 28)
Gypsy	(July 29 - August 4)
Good News	(August 5 - 11)
Bitter Sweet	(August 12 - 18)
Mack and Mabel	(August 19 - 25)
Moiseyev Dance Company	(August 26 - Sept. 1)

1975

The Bolshoi Ballet	(June 30 - July 6)
The Odd Couple	(July 7 - 13)
Carousel	(July 14 - 20)
Funny Girl	(July 21 - 27)
Camelot	(July 28 - August 3)
Girl Crazy	(August 4 - 10)
The Wizard of Oz	(August 11 - 17)
Kiss Me, Kate	(August 18 - 24)
The Mitzi Gaynor Show	(August 25 - 31)

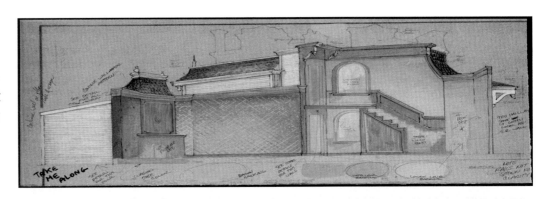

RIGHT: Grady Larkins designed some of The Muny's most elegant sets throughout the 1970s. This sketch was for *Take Me Along*, 1974.

REPERTORY

1970S

1976

Fiddler on the Roof	(July 5 - 11)
Mame	(July 12 - 18)
On the Town	(July 19 - 25)
Show Boat	(July 26 - August 1)
The King and I	(August 2 - 8)
Oliver!	(August 9 - 15)
The Baker's Wife	(August 16 -22)
Russian Festival of Music and Dance	(August 23 - 29)
1776	(August 30 - Sept. 5)

1977

Meet Me In St. Louis	(June 27 - July 3)
Hello, Dolly!	(July 4 - 10)
Finian's Rainbow	(July 11 - 17)
Guys and Dolls	(July 18 - 24)
Wonderful Town	(July 25 - 31)
The Sound of Music	(August 1 - 7)
Kismet	(August 8 - 14)
Porgy and Bess	(August 15 - 21)
Sweet Charity	(August 22 - 28)
Chicago	(August 29 - Sept. 4)

1978

Seven Brides for Seven Brothers	(June 19 - 25)
Annie	(June 26 - July 9)
Man of La Mancha	(July 10 - 16)
Oklahoma!	(July 17 - 23)
The Music Man	(July 24 - 30)
Madame Butterfly	(July 31 - August 6)
Damn Yankees	(August 7 - 13)
Nureyev with the Dutch National Ballet	(August 14 - 20)
Peter Pan	(August 21 - 27)

1979

My Fair Lady	(June 25 - July 1)
A Funny Thing Happened on the Way to the Forum	(July 2 - 8)
Shenandoah	(July 9 - 15)
Brigadoon	(July 16 - 22)
The Desert Song	(July 23 - 29)
Carousel	(July 30 - August 5)
Tom Sawyer	(August 6 - 12)
Sugar	(August 13 - 19)
Ballroom	(August 20 - 26)
Bells are Ringing	(August 27 - Sept. 2)

THE BOX OFFICE TERRAZZO
1971

From The Muny Archive

Photo by Larry Williams, of the St. Louis Post-Dispatch

LEFT: WINNING DESIGN – "Miss Nancy Day holding her prize-winning design for a terrazzo floor to be placed in front of the Municipal Opera box office in Forest Park. With Miss Day in the area under construction is Howard Baer, a past president of the Municipal Opera Association, who presented the $150 first prize to the Washington University sophomore."

Photo and cutline from the St. Louis Post-Dispatch, May 28, 1971.

PAT ST. JAMES AND ANYTHING GOES, 1972

ANN MILLER

From The Muny Archive

PAT ST. JAMES

From The Muny Archive

On opening night of *Anything Goes* in 1972, star Ann Miller experienced a backstage accident that left her unable to continue the performance. The second act was canceled and by the next evening, a St. Louis woman, a member of the ensemble, went on in her place. Pat St. James earned high praise from the critics and a standing ovation for her performance as Reno Sweeney. Ms. Miller was unable to complete the run, and returned to The Muny in 1984, in *Sugar Babies*.

DANCE COMPANIES 1970S AND '80S

Sol Hurok was considered an impresario, a flamboyant talent manager, and the founder of the booking company, Sol Hurok Presents. In the 1970s and '80s, Margot Fonteyn, Rudolf Nureyev and Mikhail Baryshnikov played The Muny through Hurok's aegis.

1970
Moiseyev Dance Company (Sept. 1 - 6)

1971
The Stuttgart Ballet (June 14 - 20)

1972
Ukrainian Dance Company (July 18 - 23)

1973
The Bolshoi Ballet (August 13 - 19)

1974
Moiseyev Dance Company (August 26 - Sept. 1)

1975
The Bolshoi Ballet (June 30 - July 6)

1976
Russian Festival of Music and Dance (August 23 - 29)

1978
Nureyev with Dutch National Ballet (August 14 - 20)

1983
Mikhail Baryshnikov in
An Evening of Classical Ballet (August 8 - 14)

1986
La Scala Ballet in Franco Zeffirelli's
Swan Lake (July 7 - 13)

Rudolf Nureyev on The Muny's rehearsal platform, with the Dutch National Ballet, 1978.

David Henschel Phtography

David Henschel Phtography

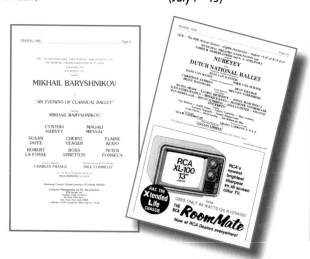

ABOVE: Nureyev, on stage at The Muny
LEFT: Title pages from a few dance companies.

As early as 1968, Muny audiences were eased into the idea of The Muny as a concert venue. Herb Alpert and the Tijuana Brass shocked the more staid Muny-goers, and when the concert experiment continued through the '70s, more than one bewildered patron wrote letters to the editors of the Post-Dispatch. Nevertheless, The Muny continued with non-traditional programming, running a series of one-star shows and pop concerts into the early 1990s.

1968
Herb Alpert and the Tijuana Brass   (August 4)

1970
The Red Skelton Show   (June 27)
An Evening with Burt Bacharach   (July 1 - 2)
The Engelbert Humperdinck Show   (July 4)

1971
The Glen Campbell Show   (July 12 - 13)
Diahann Carroll with John Denver   (July 14)
The Jim Nabors Show   (July 15 - 16)
The Jimmy Durante Show   (July 17)
The Robert Goulet Show   (July 18)

1972
Carpenters present
    Skiles and Henderson   (July 10)
The Big Show of 1936   (July 11)
Dinah Shore with Peter Nero   (July 12)
The Pearl Bailey Show   (July 13)
The Sonny and Cher Show   (July 14 - 15)
The New 1972 Jim Nabors Show   (July 16)

1973
The Carroll O'Connor Show   (June 29 - July 1)

1976
New York Philharmonic
    Conducted by Leonard Bernstein   (June 26)
New York Philharmonic
    Conducted by Andre Kostelanetz   (June 27)
Al Hirt's *Impressions of New Orleans*   (June 28 - 30)
Grand Ole Muny Opry   (July 1 - 2)
Burt Bacharach and Anthony Newley   (July 3 - 4)

1980
Richard Rodgers: A Man and His Music   (June 20)

1994
Gateway to the Gold: A Musical Celebration!   (June 29)

1995
An Evening of Operetta
    featuring *The Merry Widow*   (June 28 - 29)

1996
The Desert Song in Concert   (July 2 - 3)

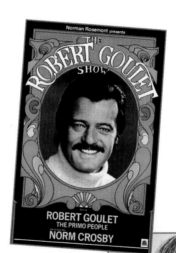

LEFT: A promotional flier from Robert Goulet's one-man show, 1971.
BELOW: A publicity photo for *The Sonny and Cher Show,* 1972. The 8:15 show sold out almost immediately, and a midnight concert was added.

Artifacts from The Muny Archive

Direct From Broadway

Back in the day, Broadway theatres traditionally felt a severe slump during the summer months. In a happy compromise, some of those shows were persuaded to close down for a couple of weeks in New York in order to play The Muny.

Hello, Dolly!	1968 and 1971
Promises, Promises	1970
Applause	1971
Follies	1972
Seesaw	1973
Irene	1973
Over Here!	1974
Chicago	1977

FOLLIES, 1972

SCENES FROM the Broadway musical hit, "Follies," which will open Muny Opera's season Monday with the original Broadway production. Above, the "Ben's Folly" number. Right, Gene Nelson dances. Then, Alexis Smith and John McMartin. Far right, Yvonne DeCarlo comforts McMartin.

Broadway's 'Follies' Opening Muny Opera Season

From the St. Louis Post-Dispatch

From The Muny Archive

Although *Follies* ran for over 500 performances in New York and won seven Tonys, it was not a financial success. It embarked on a national tour, playing The Muny in July of 1972, and then Los Angeles. The latter production ran from July through October of 1972, and the tour stopped there. ABOVE RIGHT, original cast member Yvonne De Carlo is photographed at The Muny's backstage cantina... in a fur coat...in St. Louis...in July.

FLORENCE HENDERSON – Muny Favorite

From The Muny Archive

Florence Henderson made her Muny debut in 1968, as Maria in *The Sound of Music*. She made four more Muny apperances: *Bells are Ringing* (1979), *South Pacific* (1980), *Richard Rodgers: A Man and His Music* (1980), and *Annie Get Your Gun* (1981).

ABOVE: One of Ms. Henderson's early headshots.
RIGHT: As Ella in *Bells are Ringing*, 1979.

Photo by David Henschel

PRE-BROADWAY PRODUCTIONS

The 1970s saw a trend originating from New York. Shows slated to open soon first toured in selected cities as a tryout and refining opportunity. Although not all of the shows made it to Broadway, The Muny audiences enjoyed seeing shows before they hit the Big Apple.

Lorelei	1973
Gigi	1973
Good News	1974
Mack and Mabel	1974
Gypsy (revival)	1974
The Baker's Wife	1976
The King and I (revival)	1976
Fiddler on the Roof (revival)	1976
Hello, Dolly! (revival)	1977
Seven Brides for Seven Brothers	1978
Gypsy (revival)	1989

Yul Brynner recreated his iconic Broadway and film role in *The King and I* at The Muny in 1976.

From The Muny Achive

BETTY GRABLE: HOMETOWN GIRL MAKES GOOD

Film star and wartime pinup girl Betty Grable made two Muny appearances, 45 years apart. Her first was as one of the Holland Kiddies in *The Red Mill* (1926). She returned in 1971, with *This is Show Business*, in the company of Chita Rivera, Dorothy Lamour, Don Ameche, Dennis Day and Rudy Vallée. A native St. Louisan, Miss Grable left the city at age 12 with her mother, seeking (and finding) success in the film industry.

RIGHT: A promotional flier for the all-star production, *This is Show Business.*

BELOW: Betty Grable's credit for *The Red Mill*.

THE HOLLAND KIDDIES
GIRLS AND BOYS

Arvola Oxman	Jane Clark	Junior Artz	Bobby Hauseman
Audrey Gleeson	Dolores Weil	Maxine Gloctner	Doris Frank
Jane Haberle	Patti Powers	Laura Brasch	Katherine Modest
Evelyn Matthews	Georgia Lee Dishman	Bobby Dickman	Lynn Pavit
Lavern Saul	Nadine Beardsley	Betty Carato	Lorraine Krueger
Dolly Popp	Gladys Stenman	Lewella Green	Edith Owen
Audrey Budd	Elizabeth Pogue	Edward Beckemeier	Junior Donahue
Louise Corcoran	Baby Bergt	Eunice Norris	Susan Renard
Betty Grable	Dorothy Olsen	Marjorie Gregory	Samuel Mayes
Mary Curotto	Lola Layton	John Pohlman	Gretchen Kimmel

Program continued on second page following

68

From The Muny Archive

IRENE, 1973

When Debbie Reynolds starred in *Irene*, she famously stepped to the edge of the stage and entertained the audience during a rain delay.

From The Muny Archive

TAKE ME ALONG, 1974

Hollywood song-and-dance man Gene Kelly kicked up his heels in The Muny's 1974 production of *Take Me Along*.

From The Muny Archive

THE MUSIC MAN, 1978

In 1978, Tony Randall marched into River City and saved the town from the "terrible, terrible trouble" in which it found itself.

AMERICA in the 1980s

- Average life expectancy for men was 70.0 years.
- Average cost of a gallon of gas was $1.19.
- Average cost for a loaf of bread was 50 cents.
- Average cost for a new home was $68,700.
- Average cost of a new car was $7,200.
- Average annual wage was $19,500.
- The top 5 TV shows of 1980 were: *Dallas, The Dukes of Hazzard, 60 Minutes, M*A*S*H* and *The Love Boat.*
- In 1980, John Lennon was assassinated in New York City.
- The Cold War ended in 1989 when the Berlin Wall fell.
- The Energizer Bunny was born in 1989.

STATE OF THE MUNY

BIG DOINGS AT THE MUNY OPERA

"This season, they used a 1977 survey among high-school students and discovered that that particular group thinks 'opera' means grand opera, which means heavy music in a foreign language, attended by rich, older people.

"So the Muny streamlined its name.

"No, they're not going to call it the Muny Rock Opera, which might interest both high school students and geologists.

"They're calling it just "The Muny," which sounds more like a public transportation system.

"But it has been designed on a new logo, and it will no doubt become familiar, just like the substitution of numbers for those grand old telephone exchange names eventually became familiar.

"The survey didn't stop with opera, either. It also discovered that the local population had changed substantially in the last 20 years. In addition, it found that there was competition in the summertime, and that some people preferred to go to places like the movies, or the Mississippi River Festival, or Six Flags, or baseball games, or the Pops concerts…"

Joe Pollack
St. Louis Post-Dispatch
March 9, 1980

The familiar Muny logo at RIGHT was first designed in 1980.

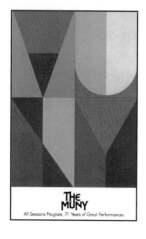

THE MUNY
All Seasons Program, 71 Years of Great Performances

THE MUNY ALL SEASONS PROGRAM
70 Years Of Great Performances

EVERYONE'S A CRITIC

Once in the newspaper, an opinion becomes carved in stone.
Here are a couple of critical critiques from the 1980s.

ST. LOUIS POST-DISPATCH   Fri., May 14, 1982   7C

Muny May Open Shows At Fox In September

By Charlene Prost
Of the Post-Dispatch Staff

Officials at the Municipal Opera and developers of the Fox Theater tentatively have agreed to use the historic building for theatrical productions starting in September.

Leon Strauss, representing the group which is reopening the Fox, said that an agreement in principle had been reached, but that final details still had to be worked out. He was optimistic that negotiations could be completed successfully within the next week.

"We are very, very close," Strauss said, "and we are actually working together as though there was an agreement already."

Strauss said that Frank C. Pierson, an associate of the Muny, had been working with Raymond Shepardson, manager of the Fox, to bring theatrical productions there starting in September.

The old motion picture theater, at 527 North Grand Boulevard, currently is being renovated and is expected to be ready for use in the fall.

Strauss said that if an agreement was signed with the Muny, the theater season at the Fox would open Sept. 7 with a production of "Barnum," a musical about P.T. Barnum, the 19th-century showman and circus operator.

For a show in September, arrangements ought to begin now, theater sources said.

Edwin R. "Bill" Culver III, general manager of the Muny, said: "We are negotiating a lot of details right now, and I am hopeful we can resolve them in the very near future to everyone's satisfaction."

Sources said discussions had been under way for months on how the Muny, which produces a series of musical shows each summer in Forest Park, might fill a "winter" season into the Fox's 4,500-seat auditorium.

A stumbling block reportedly has been the Muny's desire to own part of the building. Strauss is said to have opposed this.

The Fox is owned by the city's Planned Industrial Expansion Authority, which has leased the building to Strauss' developers.

The authority also has approved issuing up to $2 million in tax-exempt revenue bonds so that Strauss can "borrow" that money to assist in the big renovation.

Shepardson has said that he wants the Fox to offer a variety of entertainment, including musicals and other theatrical productions, and that he hopes an agreement can be reached with the Muny.

The Muny's plans for the 1980s included a year-round season. By September of 1982, Muny productions at the Fox were were a real venture.

Photo by David M. Henschel

Namath Out Of His League In 'Abner'

By Judy J. Newmark
Of the Post-Dispatch Staff

Suppose Joel Grey got it into his head that the thing he'd really like to do, to cap a career of triumph after triumph on the musical stage, was — to become an NFL quarterback.

What do you suppose would happen to him, the man who won renown as the emcee in "Cabaret"? Well, *if* he could get someone to go along with this notion, and *if* he emerged from scrimmage with his lively little legs still in two lively little pieces, then he might have one whole minute of play before he was squashed like a bug.

This is more or less what happens to Joe Namath, who is trying the same thing in reverse. He is starring in "Li'l Abner," the current show at the Municipal Opera.

If it seems ridiculous to think of Grey passing the ball, then you ought to hear Namath sing a love duet. Let's put it this way: For this production, a lot of livestock is brought onto the Muny stage. When it comes to voices, the squealing piglet gives Namath some solid competition.

What he lacks as a singer, Namath lacks as an actor and dancer, too. He does have a really nice smile, which is fixed on his face in a manner that is probably meant to convey charm but eventually starts looking more and more like Novocain.

Karen Elshout/Post-Dispatch
Joe Namath as Lil' Abner pursued by Misty Rowe as Daisy Mae.

He also bears some physical resemblance to the handsome hillbilly. But that's not much to go on — definitely not enough to show "feelings." Okay, so he's not a very sophisticated character, a cartoon character in fact. Even a cartoon is entitled to an occasional lightbulb above its head. Namath's Abner never manages

enough spark for a birthday candle.

Director Stockton Briggle may have sensed that a leading man who doesn't sing, dance or act might have certain limitations. Maybe he tried to help by making sure nobody else on hand looks a whole lot better. As Daisy Mae, Misty Rowe is physically perfect, the cartoon come to life. Well, nearly to life. She certainly does breathe — you hear that, loud and clear, every time she tries to speak or, worse, sing.

A few performers, notably Art Ostrin as Evil Eye Fleagle and Thomas Lee Sinclair as Marryin' Sam, get into the spirit of Grady Larkins' amusing, comic strip set design. They make their characters big caricatures. But most of the others give another kind of cartoon performance — loud, messy, too sloppy to be funny.

On top of everything else, there is "Li'l Abner" itself, a show that includes topical jokes about the Eisenhower administration. Johnny Mercer and Gene de Paul wrote the bland, big-show score. Maybe if they had given "Li'l Abner" a rockabilly score, for example, it would have sounded like something special. The way it is, it sounds as much like New York or Timbuktu as Al Capp's Dogpatch.

There seems little point in doing this show at all, unless, of course, it was chosen as a vehicle for Namath. And there is something very distasteful about the whole idea of interchangeable celebrity, exploiting one kind of prominence to achieve another. It says that craft, training, talent count for nothing. The only thing that counts is fame. That, of course, is precisely what Namath offers. Period.

Post-Dispatch theater critic Judith Newmark remarked: "What he lacks as singer, Namath lacks as an actor and dancer, too."

A Coarse Line?

I had the misfortune of attending the opening night of the Muny to see "A Chorus Line," which should have been called "A Coarse Line" because that's exactly what it was.

I was with 47 people from our church whose only transportation was a rented bus. Had I my own car I would have left in short order and not sat through two hours of insulting vulgarity.

From the title of the show, I had thought I was in for an evening of good, entertaining singing and dancing. Well, the singing voices were beautiful and the dancing at the end of the show was excellent. They were all very talented people on that stage. It was just a shame that the words set to the music and the dialogue were common and vulgar.

I never thought the Muny would stoop to such base standards. And those in my group whom I talked with were of the same opinion.

An unhappy Muny-goer said of the Pulitzer Prize-winning *A Chorus Line*: "I never thought The Muny would stoop to such base standards."

Photo by David M. Henschel

REPERTORY
1980s

1980

South Pacific	(June 23 - 29)
The Debbie Reynolds Show	(June 30 - July 6)
Carnival	(July 7 - 13)
Bye Bye Birdie	(July 14 - 20)
Little Me	(July 21 - 27)
Li'l Abner	(July 28 - August 3)
Cinderella	(August 4 - 10)
Al Jolson, Tonight!	(August 11 - 17)
The Merry Widow	(August 18 - 24)
Sugar Babies	(August 25 - Sept. 7)

1981

Kiss Me, Kate	(June 15 - 21)
Flower Drum Song	(June 22 - 28)
George M!	(June 29 - July 5)
Camelot	(July 6 - 12)
Annie Get Your Gun	(July 13 - 19)
Show Boat	(July 20 - 26)
A Grand Night for Singing	(July 27 - August 2)
Hans Christian Andersen	(August 3 - 9)
How to Succeed in Business Without Really Trying	(August 10 -16)
The Mitzi Gaynor Show	(August 17 - 23)
A Chorus Line	(August 24 - 30)

1982

Fiddler on the Roof	(June 21 - 27)
The Unsinkable Molly Brown	(June 28 - July 4)
The Sound of Music	(July 5 - 11)
Gigi	(July 12 - 18)
Anything Goes	(July 19 - 25)
West Side Story	(July 26 - August 1)
Grease	(August 2 - 8)
They're Playing Our Song	(August 9 - 15)
Where's Charley?	(August 16 - 22)
The Wiz	(August 23 - 29)
A Chorus Line	(August 30 - Sept. 5)

1983

The King and I	(June 20 - 26)
Promises, Promises	(June 27 - July 3)
Can-Can	(July 4 - 10)
Annie	(July 11 - 17)
Pal Joey	(July 18 - 24)
High Button Shoes	(July 25 -31)
Man of La Mancha	(August 1 - 7)
Mikhail Baryshnikov in *"An Evening of Classical Ballet"*	(August 8 - 14)
Camelot	(August 15 - 21)
The Pirates of Penzance	(August 22 - 28)
I Do! I Do!	(August 29 - Sept. 4)

1984

The Music Man	(July 9 - 15)
Dream Street	(July 16 - 22)
Funny Girl	(July 23 - 29)
Oklahoma!	(July 30 - August 5)
Sugar Babies	(August 6 - 12)
Sleeping Beauty	(August 13 - 19)

1985

A Chorus Line	(June 17 - 23)
My Fair Lady	(June 24 - 30)
Festival on Ice	(July 8 - July 14)
Bob Fosse's Dancin'	(July 15 - 21)
Jesus Christ Superstar	(July 22 - 28)
Evita	(August 5 - 11)
42nd Street	(August 12 - 18)

Repertory

1986

42nd Street	(June 16 - 22)
Singin' in the Rain	(June 23 - 29)
Show Boat	(July 14 - 20)
La Cage aux Folles	(July 21 - 27)
Pippin	(July 28 - August 3)
Gentlemen Prefer Blondes	(August 4 - 10)
Shenandoah	(August 11 - 17)
The Apple Tree (The Diary of Adam & Eve) and Joseph and the Amazing Technicolor® Dreamcoat	(August 18 - 24)

1987

The Sound of Music	(June 15 - 21)
My One and Only	(June 22 - 28)
Cats	(July 6 - July 12)
Fiddler on the Roof	(July 13 - 19)
Peter Pan	(July 20 - 26)
Around the World in 80 Days	(August 3 - 9)
Big River	(August 10 - 16)

1988

The Music Man	(June 20 - 26)
Porgy and Bess	(July 11 - 17)
Drood! (The Mystery of Edwin Drood)	(July 18 - 24)
Oliver!	(July 25 - 31)
Man of La Mancha	(August 1 - 7)
Grease	(August 8 -14)
Carousel	(August 15 - 21)

1989

A Chorus Line	(June 5 - 11)
Gypsy	(June 19 - 25)
The King and I	(July 17 - 23)
Evita	(July 24 - 30)
Godspell	(July 31 - August 6)
The Unsinkable Molly Brown	(August 14 - 20)
Annie	(August 21 - 27)

The Winter Series

Beginning with *Barnum*, which opened on September 7, 1982, The Muny and the Fox Theatre co-produced touring Broadway shows at the Fox for 10 seasons. Presented was an eclectic slate of dramas and comedies, musicals and straight plays, star turns and international dance companies. The final show of the series was *The Secret Garden*, which closed on May 10, 1992.

1982-1983

Barnum	(Sept. 7 - 19)
Hello, Dolly!	(Oct. 19 - 24)
Sugar Babies	(Dec. 14 - 19,
	Dec. 28 - Jan. 1)
Bob Fosse's Dancin'	(Jan. 26 - 30)
Amadeus	(Feb. 1 - 6)
Your Arms Too Short to Box with God	(Feb. 15 - 20)
Evita	(March 8 - 13)
Lena Horne: The Lady and Her Music	(April 8 - 17)
Peter Pan	(May 3 - 8)
Porgy and Bess	(May 17 - 22)
Sophisticated Ladies	(May 31 - June 5)
* Mass Appeal	(June 7 - 19)

1983 - 1984

Bob Fosse's Dancin'	(Sept. 20 - 25)
Fiddler on the Roof	(Oct. 25 - 30)
Evita	(Nov. 22 - 27)
Woman of the Year	(Dec. 9 - 18)
A Christmas Carol	(Dec. 20 - 22)
Beethoven's 10th	(Jan. 10 - 15)
The Wiz	(Feb. 7 - 12)
* A Soldier's Play	(Feb. 14 - 26)
Joseph and the Amazing Technicolor® Dreamcoat	(Feb. 28 - March 4)
* Crimes of the Heart	(March 13 - 18)
* Agnes of God	(March 20 - April 1)
* Oliver!	(April 3 - 8)
42nd Street	(April 25 - May 13)
The King and I	(May 17 - June 17)

1984 - 1985

* Torch Song Trilogy	(Oct. 30 - Nov. 4)
* 'Night, Mother	(Nov. 13 - 25)
Zorba	(Nov. 28 - Dec. 9)
Gigi	(Jan. 15 - 20)
* Pop!! Goes the Music!	(Jan. 24 - Feb. 6)
* Ain't Misbehavin'	(Feb. 26 - March 10)
* Brighton Beach Memoirs	(March 19 - 30)
La Cage aux Folles	(April 16 - 28)
* Ceremonies in Dark Old Men	(April 23 - May 5)
Sing, Mahalia, Sing	(May 29 - June 2)

1985 - 1986

* Corpse	(Sept. 3 - 8)
* Noises Off	(Sept. 13 - 22)
* Old Times	(Oct. 19 - 26)
The Tap Dance Kid	(Jan. 21 - 26)
Dreamgirls	(Feb. 4 - 9)
My One and Only	(March 5 - 9)
* A Coupla White Chicks Sitting Around Talking	(March 11 - 16)
* Annie	(April 8 - 13)
Brigadoon	(April 29 - May 4)
* The Best Little Whorehouse in Texas	(May 6 -11)

1986-1987

Camelot	(Sept. 2 - 7)
* The Late Great Ladies of Blues & Jazz	(Sept. 23 -28)
Moiseyev Dance Company	(Sept. 30 - Oct. 5)
* Doubles	(Oct. 14 - 19)
* Legends	(Oct. 29 - Nov. 9)
* Do Black Patent Leather Shoes Really Reflect Up?	(Nov. 14)
Cats	(Nov. 18 - 23)
On the Twentieth Century	(Jan. 6 -11)
* I'm Not Rappaport	(Jan. 20 - 25)
* Biloxi Blues	(Feb. 24 - March 1)
* Arsenic and Old Lace	(March 24 - 29)
* Social Security	(April 21 - 26)

* Indicates that the show was presented at the American Theatre. All others at the Fox.

The Winter Series

1987 - 1988

* Song and Dance	(Sept. 8 - 13)
* The Odd Couple	(Sept. 15 - 20)
* I Never Sang for My Father	(Nov. 3 - 8)
The Wizard of Oz	(Dec. 27 - Jan. 3)
South Pacific	(Feb. 2 - 7)
Me and My Girl	(March 22 - 27)
Cats	(April 5 - 10)

1988 - 1989

Cabaret	(Sept. 27 - Oct. 2)
Can-Can	(Nov. 1 - 6)
Dreamgirls	(Jan. 3 - 8)
Elvis: A Musical Celebration	(Feb. 7 - 12)
Les Misérables	(March 14 - 19)
Into the Woods	(April 4 - 9)

1989 - 1990

** American Ballet Theatre	(Oct. 17 - 22)
Starlight Express	(Dec. 5 - 10)
Fiddler on the Roof	(Jan. 2 - 7)
Chess	(Feb. 20 - 25)
Anything Goes	(March 6 - 11)
Peter Pan	(April 3 - 8)
Les Misérables	(May 8 - 13)
Ken Hill's The Phantom of the Opera	(May 29 - June 3)

1990 - 1991

The Fantasticks	(Oct. 9 - 14)
Cats	(Nov. 6 - 11)
The Music of Andrew Lloyd Webber	(Dec. 4 - 9)
Big River	(Jan. 15 - 20)
Grand Hotel	(Feb. 26 - March 3)
Meet Me In St. Louis	(April 30 - May 5)
Ziegfeld: A Night at the Follies	(May 28 - June 2)

1991 - 1992

Buddy	(Oct. 22 - 27)
Cats	(Dec. 3 - 8)
City of Angels	(Jan. 28 - Feb. 2)
A Chorus Line	(March 3 - 8)
Les Misérables	(March 31 - April 5)
Lost In Yonkers	(April 21 - 26)
The Secret Garden	(May 5 - 10)

* Indicates the show was presented at the American Theatre.
** Indicates the show was presented at the Kiel.
All others at the Fox.

LEFT: Program cover and ads for The Muny's Winter Series at the Fox.

THAT'S THE TICKET!

In the earliest days of The Muny, tickets were sold at Kieselhorst's Piano Company, located at 1007 Olive Street in downtown St. Louis. In 1927, the Quonset hut seen behind the main structure just to the left of middle in the photo below, was added for dressing room space. It is probable that the wooden buildings below, which served as general offices as well as the summer box office, were built around the same time.

From The Muny Archive

From The Muny Archive

For many years, The Muny Box Office was located in a kiosk in the Arcade Building.

From The Muny Archive

From The Muny Archive

In the 1950s and beyond, season tickets were sold in The Muny's administrative building.

In 1984, a heated indoor area was added to the Box Office structure, making the purchasing process more comfortable for cold-weather ticket buyers.

CONCERTS
STARFEST

In 1984, the Starfest Series was initiated. These ran from 1984 through 1990, and were often co-produced with Contemporary Productions.

1984

Al Jarreau	(June 22)
Red Skelton	(June 25)
Time to Remember	
The Original Four Aces with	
The Four Freshmen/	
The Four Lads/	
The Ink Spots	(June 26)
Gershwin: A Celebration of	
Music and Dance Festival	(June 28)
Linda Ronstadt with	
Nelson Riddle	
and his Orchestra	(July 2)
Wayne Newton	(July 5 - 6)
Bob Hope and Shirley Jones	(July 7)
Little River Band with Poco	(August 22)
Crosby, Stills & Nash	(August 23)
Let the Good Times Roll	
With Rick Nelson,	
Wolfman Jack, Lesley Gore,	
Bobby Vee, The Coasters,	
The Crystals,	
Rockin' Robins	
Rhythm Kings	(August 24)
Merle Haggard	(August 25)
George Jones with the Jones Boys	
and Earl Thomas Conley	(August 26)
Waylon Jennings and Jessi Colter	(August 31)
James Taylor and Randy Newman	(September 4)
The Go-Go's	(September 6)

1985

Kenny Loggins	(June 2)
Santana	(June 7)
Al Jarreau	(July 30)
The Beach Boys	(August 3)
Alabama	(August 24)
Sting	(September 1)

1986

Jimmy Buffett	(June 6)
The Beach Boys	(June 7)
The Moody Blues	(July 1)
Julian Lennon	(July 2)
Starship	(July 3)
Whitney Houston	(September 1)
Kenny Loggins	(September 5)

1987

The Partland Brothers	
and the Moody Blues	(June 29)
Chicago	(July 1)
Neil Young and Crazy Horse	(August 17)

1988

Hank Williams, Jr.	(May 29)
Robert Plant	(June 4)
Bob Dylan	(June 17)
Bruce Hornsby and Pat McLaughlin	(July 2)
Steve Winwood	(July 7)
Chicago and Henry Lee Summer	(August 23)
REO Speedwagon	(August 26)
An Evening with James Taylor	(September 2)
Barry Manilow Concert Tour	(September 3)
The Moody Blues	(September 7)
Huey Lewis and the News	(September 8)

CONCERTS
STARFEST CNTD.

1989

The Doobie Brothers	(June 16)
Rod Stewart	(June 27)
Steve Miller	(July 7)
Patti LaBelle	(July 13)
Don Henley, Edie Brickell and the New Bohemians	(August 8)
Bob Dylan	(August 9)
Al Jarreau and Take Six	(August 12)
Stevie Nicks and the Hooters	(Sept. 14)

1990

Heart and Giant	(June 22)
Milli Vanilli, Young MC, and Seduction	(July 16)
Chicago and Poco	(July 17)
The B-52s, Ziggy Marley and The Melody Makers	(July 19)
Don Henley	(July 20)
Kenny G and Michael Bolton	(August 20)
Crosby, Stills & Nash	(August 21)
Bonnie Raitt with Charles Brown and the Jeff Healey Band	(August 22)
Alabama with Clint Black	(August 24)
Linda Ronstadt with Aaron Neville and the Neville Brothers	(Sept. 16)

1991

The Allman Brothers Band and Little Feat	(August 9)
The Moody Blues with Kansas	(August 29)

The graphics on this page are from a 1984 marketing brochure.

Photo by David M. Henschel

ANNIE GET YOUR GUN, 1981

Florence Henderson as Annie Oakley is slack-jawed upon meeting Frank Butler (Ron Husmann) in *Annie Get Your Gun,* 1981. Ms. Henderson made a total of five Muny appearances.

GREASE, 1982

Grease made its Muny debut in 1982, and has played there an additional five times. That first production starred Laurie Stephenson and Mark Martino.

Photo by David M. Henschel

Photo by David M. Henschel

FUNNY GIRL, 1984

Juliet Prowse starred as funny girl Fanny Brice, in The Muny's 1984 production.

AMERICA in the 1990s

- Average life expectancy for men was 71.8 years.
- Average cost of a gallon of gas was $1.34.
- Average cost for a loaf of bread was 70 cents.
- Average cost for a new home was $123,000.
- Average cost of a new car was $16,950.
- Average annual wage was $28,960.
- The top five TV shows of 1990 were: *Cheers, 60 Minutes,*
- *Roseanne, A Different World* and *The Cosby Show.*
- The Soviet Union dissolved in 1991 when Mikhail Gorbechev resigned.
- In 1995, O.J. Simpson was found not guilty of double murder.
- In 1997, British scientists cloned a sheep known as Dolly.

STATE OF THE MUNY

"Revivals are everywhere. *Damn Yankees* and *My Fair Lady* in New York. *Carousel* in London and opening on Broadway later this month.

"Why should St. Louis be any different?

"Well, it isn't, as a look at the spring and summer seasons here in River City will establish...

"It would be easy to attack the theaters for continuing to bring back old musicals – some good, some bad, some indifferent – but it would be a real cheap shot because there just isn't anything else out there. Anything new, or recent, or on a national production.

"So it would be easy to bash The Muny, or Stages, or the Fox for the months ahead, but it would be unfair. As the old saloon sign says, 'Don't shoot the piano player. He's doing the best he can.'"

Joe Pollack, St. Louis Post-Dispatch
February 27, 1994

PHYLLIS DILLER, 1992

39 Again

Phyllis Diller, one of The Muny's "most wanted seniors," being handcuffed Thursday at a birthday party stunt sponsored by The Muny. Fans sang "Happy Birthday" to the comic, who turns 75 today. Diller will appear in "The Wizard of Oz" at The Muny next week.

Wes Paz/Post-Dispatch

Internationally-famed funny lady Phyllis Diller made her Muny debut as the Wicked Witch in *The Wizard of Oz,* 1992. As part of the publicity efforts for that musical, Ms. Diller allowed herself to be "arrested," as Zsa Zsa Gabor had been earlier that year for slapping a policeman. Phyllis celebrated her 75th birthday while at The Muny, coinciding with The Muny's own 75th season, and returned to play the wicked Stepmother in *Cinderella* in 1995.

REPERTORY

1990s

1990

West Side Story	(June 25 - July 1)
Jesus Christ Superstar	(July 2 - 8)
Bye Bye Birdie	(July 9 - 15)
Cinderella on Ice	(July 23 - 29)
Brigadoon	(July 30 - August 5)
No, No, Nanette	(August 6 - 12)
Little Shop of Horrors	(August 13 - 19)

1991

It's Delightful, It's Delovely, It's Cole Porter!	(June 10 - 16)
Kiss Me, Kate	(June 17 - 23)
Hans Christian Andersen	(July 8 - 14)
42nd Street	(July 15 - 21)
I Do! I Do!	(July 22 - 28)
Mame	(July 29 - August 4)
My Fair Lady	(August 12 - 18)

1992

South Pacific	(June 22 - 28)
Pump Boys and Dinettes	(July 6 - 12)
Show Boat	(July 13 - 19)
The Wizard of Oz	(July 20 - 26)
Hello, Dolly!	(July 27 - August 2)
George M!	(August 3 - 9)
The Music of Andrew Lloyd Webber	(August 10 - 16)

1993

The Sound of Music	(June 21 - 27)
Annie Get Your Gun	(July 5 - 11)
Grease	(July 12 - 18)
Peter Pan	(July 19 - 25)
Fiddler on the Roof	(July 26 - August 1)
Oliver!	(August 2 - 8)
Oklahoma!	(August 9 - 15)

1994

The King and I	(June 20 - 26)
Ain't Misbehavin'	(July 4 - 10)
Cats	(July 11 - 17)
Annie	(July 18 - July 24)
Seven Brides for Seven Brothers	(July 25 - 31)
Meet Me In St. Louis	(August 1 - 7)
The Music Man	(August 8 - 14)

1995

The Music of Andrew Lloyd Webber	(June 19 - 25)
Man of La Mancha	(July 3 - 9)
Cinderella	(July 10 - 16)
Singin' in the Rain	(July 17 - 23)
Godspell	(July 24 - 30)
Camelot	(July 31 - August 6)
West Side Story	(August 7 - 13)

1996

My Fair Lady	(June 17 - 23)
Jesus Christ Superstar	(June 24 - 30)
Little Shop of Horrors	(July 8 - 14)
Sleeping Beauty	(July 15 - 21)
Guys and Dolls	(July 22 - 28)
Evita	(July 29 - August 4)
42nd Street	(August 5 - 11)

1997

Joseph and the Amazing Technicolor® Dreamcoat	(June 16 - 22)
Funny Girl	(June 23 - 29)
Three Coins in the Fountain	(July 7 - 13)
The Wizard of Oz	(July 14 - 20)
A Chorus Line	(July 21 - 27)
South Pacific	(July 28 - August 3)
Hello, Dolly!	(August 4 - 10)

Repertory

1998

Oklahoma!	(June 15 - 21)
Bye Bye Birdie	(June 22 - 28)
The Radio City Rockettes	
Muny Spectacular	(July 6 - 12)
Peter Pan	(July 13 - 19)
Fiddler on the Roof	(July 20 - 26)
Crazy for You	(July 27 - August 2)
Damn Yankees	(August 3 - 9)

1999

Grease	(June 21 - 27)
The King and I	(July 5 - 11)
Annie	(July 12 - 18)
The Muny Goes British	(July 19 - 25)
1776	(July 26 - August 1)
Anything Goes	(August 2 - 8)
Meet Me In St. Louis	(August 9 - 15)

Just two of the many ads that ran in Muny programs, promoting snacks and sodas for sale.

Dining at The Muny
by Suzanne Corbett

"Each season, The Muny experience for tens of thousands includes concessions. Concessioners have provided patrons with refreshments for decades, which ran the gambit from cold drinks and hot dogs to chilled boxes of chocolates to pizza. Over the past 100 years, concession areas have expanded to include a broader menu and two new venues, Café One and the Culver Pavilion. Café One's grab-and-go gourmet sandwich and fresh pizza concept inspires impromptu picnics.

Suzanne Corbett

Suzanne Corbett is a food historian and writer. She is the author of three culinary books, and writes frequently for local and national publications.

Photo by Jerry Naunheim

ABOVE: The Culver Pavilion, The Muny's answer to fine pre-show dining, first opened in 1992. Named for Edwin "Bill" Culver, The Muny's former managing director, the Pavilion received a major renovation in 2007.
BELOW: Café One

Photo by Phillip Hamer

PAUL BLAKE
EXECUTIVE PRODUCER, 1990 - 2011

Paul Blake served as The Muny's Executive Producer from 1990 through 2011. His greatest contributions to The Muny include a return to Muny-produced musicals, and the introduction of several world premieres including *Roman Holiday,* and *Irving Berlin's White Christmas* which enjoyed two successful runs on Broadway. Mr. Blake is also the producer of *Beautiful: The Carole King Musical* and the revival of *Sunset Boulevard* which starred Glenn Close.

"I spent 22 of the best and happiest summers of my life at The Muny. When I began my time at The Muny, I was a young man—see the picture below — and when I ended my tenure ... well the picture at the TOP LEFT says it all. You might say I went from Romeo to Friar Laurence in 22 song-filled years, but I don't regret one hot, humid summer day of working on the rehearsal platforms or any of the myriad challenges brought my way by each of the 140 shows I and my talented team produced at the theatre.

"I love The Muny, the 30-piece orchestra, and the best musical theatre audience anywhere in this world. Happy 100th birthday and thanks for the memories."

Paul Blake

Bringing Magic To The Muny?

Bubbling with plans, Paul Blake takes over as executive producer

By Joe Pollack
Of the Post-Dispatch Staff

PAUL BLAKE looked out the window. The grass in Forest Park glistened, green as a leprechaun's jacket, in the morning rain.

"Even in the rain, I love this city," he said happily. "It meant so much to me the last time I was here — my first real job, my first credit cards, my first drivers license, my first car, my first house with a doorbell that went 'ding-dong.'

"I always had lived in apartments, like any New Yorker. You know, 'Bzzzz.' "

Blake, short and slight, with brown hair and a salt-and-pepper beard, has a little of the leprechaun in his eyes when he talks, even more of one in his enthusiastic gestures. He sat in The Muny's board room last week, his first day in his new office in his new job as executive producer of The Muny, and like any theatrical producer, he talked of theatrical magic. He wore a pink shirt with a trademark on the pocket, a green tie with a pheasant pattern and a plaid jacket, and he was rarely still, bouncing in his chair, spreading his arms on the table, leaning forward, stretching backward.

Blake's enthusiasm is contagious, and as he talked of Muny Past, Muny Present and Muny Yet to Come, his vision spread far beyond Forest Park. He was speculating, even dreaming a little, but he talked of a resident company, and of using the giant stage to the utmost, and of becoming a home for musical theater production.

These things are down the road, of course, but as Blake looks to something as close as the 1990 season — starting 11 weeks from Monday — he speaks with the same enthusiasm.

Paul Blake, new executive producer of The Muny.

Wayne Crosslin/Post-Dispatch

THE MUNY "REP"

Paul Blake established an informal repertory company of favorite performers who starred in various roles throughout his tenure. A few of them are pictured BELOW.

GEORGIA ENGEL   BRUCE ADLER   VICTORIA MALLORY   LEE ROY REAMS

THE 75TH SEASON CELEBRATION, 1993

When The Muny celebrated its 75th Season in1993, Miss Hullings and the Muny stagehands found themselves in an unlikely partnership. While Miss Hullings' bakers made 10,000 pieces of birthday cake for the audience, the stagehands designed a ceremonial replica for an on-stage tribute.

PICTURED, IN ALPHABETICAL ORDER: Steve Boianoff, Clarence Conley, Rocco Dattoli, Ron Eberhardt, Oliver Hoffstetter, Emmett McDonald, Tim McDonald, Bruce Mourning, Steve Seago, Don Shenbrook, Richard Shetley, Rick Shetley, George Spies, Dave Stone and Kevin Whalen.

Photo by Jim Herren

ON YOUR TOES

REMEMBERING GEMZE DE LAPPE   BY GIA VALENTI

Gemze de Lappe was a Broadway dancer and a choreographer, who choreographed 16 shows at The Muny between 1993 and 2009. Ms. de Lappe was also a featured dancer in The Muny's 1954 *Call Me Madam*. Gia Valenti, a frequent member of The Muny's dance ensemble, remembers her friend and mentor.

"Gemze was the most beautiful and legendary choreographer I had the opportunity to work with and learn from. As a young dancer, I'd walk up to the West Platform knowing I was about to spend 10 days of blood, sweat and tears with THE Simon of Legree from the original production of *The King and I* (onstage and on screen). She cast me as Little Eva and I was beyond honored. I remember Gemze in 2006, she at the age of 84. At 10:00 a.m. she would already be there doing a full ballet barre prior to an 8-hour rehearsal on a St. Louis summer day. I am blessed to have experienced the style of Agnes de Mille through Gemze's promise to not only keep Ms. de Mille's work alive, but meticulously executed".

Gia Valenti

LESLIE DENNISTON

JOEL HIGGINS

KAREN MORROW

FRANCIS JUE

KEN PAGE

AIN'T MISBEHAVIN' 1994

Ken earned his Equity card at The Muny in 1973, performing in the singing ensemble. On Broadway, he starred as Nicely-Nicely Johnson in the all-Black revival of *Guys and Dolls,* for which he won the Theatre World Award. He earned the Drama Desk Award for his performance in *Ain't Misbehavin',* and went on to star in the original Broadway production of *Cats* as Old Deuteronomy. Ken is best known as the voice of Oogie Boogie in *The Nightmare Before Christmas.*

Photo by Jim Herren

KEN PAGE'S FIRST MUNY BIO, 1973

Kenneth Page

Michael Page, nee' Ken Page (Stewpot) attended Bishop Du Bourg High School. While there he studied voice and drama for one year and had leading roles in OLIVER, HELLO DOLLY and portrayed Tevye in FIDDLER ON THE ROOF. He is now a Sophomore majoring in Theatre at Fontbonne College. This year he portrayed Henry VIII in ROYAL GAMBIT and Preacher Haggler in DARK OF THE MOON, and plans to go on into professional theatre as a career. This is his first appearance on the Municipal Opera stage.

"The Muny is not only where I got my first vision of the theatre, but also where I started my professional career and where I've had a theatrical home for over twenty years and 36 productions. The names and faces of those I've worked with make an incredible memory quilt that keeps me warm. In my experience with many theatres, I can truthfully say there is no place else like The Muny. The heart of all the people in back and front of the great booms is what makes that so. How lucky I have been to be part of that family of love and creativity all these years. The Muny hasn't only been an important part of my career, but it has been a most wonderful part of my life."

Ken Page

OLD DEUTERONOMY, CATS, 2004

PICKERING, MY FAIR LADY, 2001
With Rosemary Murphy, as Mrs. Higgins.

THE SULTAN, ALADDIN, 2012

Photo by Jim Herren

Photo by Jim Herren

Photo by Jim Herren

Under Construction

From The Muny Archive

Turntable Renovation, 1997

In 1997, the stage was completely refloored, and the turntable updated.

Restrooms and Concession Stands, 1998

The restrooms and concession stands were modernized in 1998, as much for efficiency as for a visual update. The number of women's restrooms were almost doubled.

From The Muny Archive

From The Muny Archive

The May Plaza, 1999

The May Plaza, located on the east side of the theatre, was completed in 1999. Already a gathering place for picnics and pre-show entertainment, the plaza added an area for personalized bricks and room for more picnic tables.

THE MUNY KIDS, 1994

In 1994, two Muny Moms, Mary Hall-Ries and Helane Bernath "invented" the concept of The Muny Kids, and created a Muny tradition of young people acting as The Muny's goodwill ambassadors. The elite touring company is still known as The Muny Kids.

From The Muny Archive

AT THE PENTAGON

In 1996, The Muny Kids performed at the White House and the Pentagon.

Helane Bernath is pictured at LEFT, with Mary Hall-Ries.

A FOUNDING MOTHER REMEMBERS   BY HELANE BERNATH

"The Muny has always held a special place in my heart. As a child, my aunt would take me to The Muny – dressed in a starched summer frock and white gloves. They were always exciting, memorable experiences.

"I was thrilled when many years later my son was cast in his first of many Muny musicals. Spending a lot of time backstage admiring the talented children, Mary came up with what she called "a scathingly brilliant idea" and asked for my help in making it a reality. That, of course, is the short version.

"Having been a co-founder of the Muny Kids/Muny Teens program has been among my proudest achievements. May The Muny continue to offer children from all walks of life the opportunity to be part of an enduring theatre community for another hundred years."

Helane Bernath

THE FIRST "CROP" OF MUNY KIDS

IN ALPHABETICAL ORDER: Kyle Banahan, Karen Banks, Jesse Bernath, Brandon Bieber, Gretchen Bieber, Christa Bross, Paul A. Brotherton, Richelle Buser, Devon Cahill, Cristal Chow, Julie Covington, Melissa Davis, Candace Deanes, Michelle Dickson, Kara Driscoll, Johanna Elkana, Daniel Estrin, Marjorie Failoni, Jacqueline Fitzgerald, Elizabeth G'Sell, Marni Glovinsky, Kay Guebert, Janae Hairston, Natalie Hall, Erika Jean Hebron, Stephanie Hickman, Caroline Holmes, Dakota Houk-Jones, Lindsay Elayne Jorns, Vonna Rose King, Emily Kochan, Jake Kohut, Jessica M. Kohut, Alison Marie Koplar, Graham Kostic, Ashley Krupinski, Jodi Kuhlmann, Jacob Laws, Miguel Marling, Kathryn Mastroinni, Ryan Bell McAdams, Peter Merideth, Erin Moore, Michael Noonan, Rosie North, Amy O'Neill, Matt Ottenlips, Craig Peterson, Emilia Pettit, Anna Marie Ransom, Anna Reby, Stephanie Reuter, Heather Schmidt, Jessica Shaw, Lauren Stiehr, LaTia Thomas, Joseph Zahn, Laura Zimmer and Jamie Zuckerman.

Photo by Jim Herren

KIDS AT THE MUNY

Long before there were Muny Kids, young people played an important role at the theatre. Here are just a few photos of kids at The Muny through the years.

1947

LEFT: four-year old Janet Dunphy was not happy to learn that she was too young for The Muny's children chorus. Her older sister Judy (10) let choreographer Dan Eckley handle the situation.

Photo by the St. Louis Post-Dispatch

Photo by the St. Louis Post-Dispatch

1936

ABOVE: Rehearsal for *Babes in Toyland*, 1936.

1984

LEFT: Among those in the 1984 children's chorus of *Sleeping Beauty* were Sanjay Shastri, Ronda Levy, Robin Berger, Keri Smith and Yvonne Meyer.

From The Muny Archive

Photo by Phillip Hamer

MUNY KIDS, 2017

Today's Muny Kids frequently perform at pre-show events. Here they are entertaining the crowds at Lichtenstein Plaza.

GREATEST HITS OF THE 1990S

OLIVER! 1993

Davy Jones, the "cute" member of the pop band The Monkees, starred as Fagin in The Muny's 1993 production of *Oliver!* Jones had made his theatrical debut 30 years earlier in London as the Artful Dodger, a role he reprised on Broadway.

Photo by Jim Herren

THE WIZARD OF OZ, 1997

St. Louis' charismatic shortstop, Ozzie Smith delighted Muny audiences, playing the title role in the 1997 production of *The Wizard of Oz.*

Photo by Jim Herren

JOSEPH AND THE AMAZING TECHNICOLOR® DREAMCOAT, 1997

A St. Louis-based fan club was formed for Eric Kunze, one of The Muny's most popular leading men. Here he stars as Joseph, in *Joseph and the Amazing Technicolor® Dreamcoat*, 1997.

Photo by Jim Herren

AMERICA in the 2000s

- Average life expectancy was 77.5 years
- The Twentieth Century began on December 31, 2000.
- Y2K didn't happen. People had feared that digital life as we knew it would end on December 31, 1999, at midnight.
- Average price of a gallon of gas was $1.56.
- A Sony Playstation was $299.00
- Brad Pitt was *People* magazine's Sexiest Man Alive
- In 2000, in an election shadowed by "hanging chads," George W. Bush defeated Al Gore for the US Presidency.
- 9-11-2001 – Terrorist attacks on American soil changed the history of the United States forever.
- February 4, 2004 – Facebook was born.
- August, 2005 – Hurricane Katrina struck the Gulf Coast.
- July 21, 2007 – *Harry Potter and the Deathly Hallows* was released.
- From 1984 to 2000, the percentage of American households with computers rose from 8.2% to 51%.
- By 2010, 77% of all American households had a computer.
- November 4, 2008, Barack Obama was elected president.

Repertory

2000s

2000
West Side Story	(June 19 - 25)
An Evening of Richard Rodgers	(July 3 - 9)
The Sound of Music	(July 10 - 16)
White Christmas	(July 17 - 23)
A Funny Thing Happened	
on the Way to the Forum	(July 24 - 30)
Seven Brides for Seven Brothers	(July 31 - August 6)
Singin' in the Rain	(August 7 - 13)

2001
Brigadoon	(June 18 - 24)
Miss Saigon	(June 25 - July 1)
Roman Holiday	(July 9 - 15)
The Wizard of Oz	(July 16 - 22)
An Evening of Gershwin	(July 23 - 29)
My Fair Lady	(July 30 - August 5)
Evita	(August 6 - 12)

2002
A Chorus Line	(June 17 - 23)
Hooray for Hollywood!	(June 24 - 30)
How to Succeed in Business	
Without Really Trying	(July 8 - 14)
Peter Pan	(July 15 - 21)
The Fantasticks	(July 22 - 28)
Camelot	(July 29 - August 4)
Joseph and the Amazing	
Technicolor® Dreamcoat	(August 5 - 11)

2003
Fiddler on the Roof	(June 16 - 22)
Side by Side by Sondheim	(June 23 - 29)
Show Boat	(July 7 - 13)
Cinderella	(July 14 - 20)
Godspell	(July 21 - 27)
Crazy for You	(July 28 - August 3)
South Pacific	(August 4 - 10)

2004
Meet Me In St. Louis	(June 21 - 30)
Cats	(July 5 - 11)
Annie	(July 12 - 18)
Breakfast at Tiffany's	(July 19 - 25)
The Music Man	(July 26 - August 1)
Guys and Dolls	(August 2 - 8)
42nd Street	(August 9 - 15)

2005
Beauty and the Beast	(June 20 - 29)
Annie Get Your Gun	(July 4 - 10)
Jesus Christ Superstar	(July 11 - 17)
Singin' in the Rain	(July 18 - 24)
Mame	(July 25 - 31)
West Side Story	(August 1 - 7)
The Sound of Music	(August 8 - 14)

2006
The King and I	(June 19 - 25)
Aida (Elton John & Tim Rice)	(June 26 - July 2)
The Wizard of Oz	(July 6 - 16)
Gypsy	(July 17 - 23)
White Christmas	(July 24 - 30)
Oliver!	(July 31 - August 6)
Seven Brides for Seven Brothers	(August 7 - 13)

2007
Oklahoma!	(June 18 - 24)
Grease	(June 25 - July 3)
Hello, Dolly!	(July 9 - 15)
Peter Pan	(July 16 - 22)
The Pajama Game	(July 23 - 29)
Joseph and the Amazing	
Technicolor® Dreamcoat	(July 30 - August 5)
Les Misérables	(August 6 - 15)

2008

The Producers	(June 16 - 22)
High School Musical	(June 23 - July 2)
My Fair Lady	(July 7 - 13)
90 Years of Muny Magic	(July 14 - 20)
Miss Saigon	(July 21 - 27)
My One and Only	(July 28 - August 3)
Fiddler on the Roof	(August 4 - 10)

2009

42nd Street	(June 15 - 21)
Annie	(June 22 - 30)
Meet Me In St. Louis	(July 6 - 12)
Godspell	(July 13 - 19)
The Music Man	(July 20 - 26)
Camelot	(July 27 - August 2)
Hairspray	(August 3 - 9)

They were, perhaps, the most pampered trees in St. Louis. Since the 1930s, the two giant oaks that flanked the Muny stage were examined by arborists on a yearly basis, and every effort was made to keep them safe. In 2002, the burr oak on stage right was deemed unsafe and was removed. The wood from that tree was upcycled and is now the boardroom table.

TAKING A FINAL BOUGH

TEAK PHILLIPS / POST-DISPATCH

Workers slowly remove a burr oak tree Tuesday that had been growing through a portion of stage right at The Muny in Forest Park. Mulch from the tree will be used in landscaping around the amphitheater. A portion of the lumber will become a large conference table inside The Muny's offices. The tree, which had become unstable from disease, was believed to be between 250 and 300 years old.

From The St. Louis Post-Dispatch

Photo by Stephen Guebert

From The Muny Archive

ABOVE: The Post-Dispatch pays tribute to one of the mighty oaks on its way out.
FAR LEFT: The boardoom table, made from that tree.
LEFT: An arborist giving the tree a check-up in 1935.

Reseating the Theatre, 2001

From The Muny Archive

From The Muny Archive

ABOVE: In 2001, the entire floor of the auditorium was resurfaced, and the seating area reconfigured. New seats were installed, slightly larger than the previous version.
LEFT: In its earliest days, The Muny borrowed benches and folding chairs from the Parks Department.

Lichtenstein Plaza, 2003

Photo by Jim Herren

Photo by Jim Herren

The Plaza at "The Top of The Muny" behind the free seats was reconfigured and landscaped in 2003. It has become a popular area for pre-show entertainment.

MUNY TRADITIONS

FREE SEATS

From The Muny Achive

Even before the Municipal Theatre Association of St. Louis was incorporated in 1919, there were free seats. When *As You Like It,* the very first show to play on the site of today's Muny was presented, free seats were advertised on a first-come, first-served basis.

"ACCESSIBLE TO ALL"

1940

Photo from the Missouri Historical Society Collections
Photo by Ruth Cunliff Russell

COMMUNITY SERVICE TICKETS

1940

Photo from the Missouri Historical Society Collections
Photo by Ruth Cunliff Russell

ABOVE: "The Muny partners with social service and community agencies to invite under-served and special-needs audiences to attend a Muny performance, free of charge."
RIGHT: "The Muny is honored to provide wheelchair assistance facilitated by our trained usher staff."

From the 2018 Muny program.

2017

Photo by Phillip Hamer

MUNY FACTOID: Every night of the Muny season, 1,456 seats are set aside as "free seats," and every Monday night an additional 1,500 seats are reserved for charitable organizations. Roughly one-fourth of all Muny seats are given away each summer at no charge. Since The Muny's inception, an estimated 10,000,000 tickets have been distributed in this way.

Photo by Jim Herren

LES MISÉRABLES, 2007

The Muny's premiere production of *Les Misérables* thrilled audiences with its romantic sweep and tragic love story.

42ND STREET, 2009

New shows were a delight and a revelation to St. Louis theatre-goers, but the extravagant staging of classics such as *42nd Street* did not disappoint.

Photo by Jim Herren

Photo by Jim Herren

HAIRSPRAY, 2009

The Muny's first production of *Hairspray* welcomed Muny audiences "to the sixties," and to writer John Waters' colorful world.

Photo by Jim Herren

AMERICA in the 2010s

- Life expectancy in 2010 was 78.54 years.
- The average price for a new car was $29, 217.
- A third of all American homes had three or more smart phones.
- The national average wage in 2010 was $48,642.15.
- The average price for a dozen eggs was $1.27.
- The population of Las Vegas was 584,682.
- The high school graduation rate was 79%.
- There were 12,996 homicides in the US in 2010.

COMPARE

A "look back" at where we were about 100 summers ago.

AMERICA in 1920

- Average life expectancy for men was 53.5 years.
- In 1923, a Model T touring car with a self-starter cost $393.00
- Only 8% of homes had a telephone.
- The average US wage in 1920 was $3,269.40.
- The average price of a dozen eggs was 14 cents.
- The population of Las Vegas was 30.
- Only 6% of Americans had graduated from high school.
- There were about 230 reported murders in the US.

STATE OF THE MUNY

"Paul Blake will conclude his 22nd season as executive producer at The Muny by directing *Bye Bye Birdie* – the first show he ever directed at the big outdoor theater in Forest Park.

"That was in 1990.

"Blake will step down at the end of the 2011 season. His successor, Mike Isaacson, will join the Muny full-time in April. Isaacson plans to spend the summer learning the Muny's ins and outs to prepare himself for the 2012 season."

Judith Newmark
St. Louis Post-Dispatch
November 28, 2010

2015

1942

1957

The Cheshire Inn has been a Muny advertiser since its earliest days as Bill Medart's, then through it's "Olde Cheshyre" phase, to today's sleek and sophisticated incarnation. For many years, the Cheshire Inn furnished double-decker buses to transport Muny-goers from the restaurant to the theatre and back again.

Repertory

2010s

2010
Beauty and the Beast	(June 21 - 30)
Titanic: The Musical	(July 5 - 11)
Damn Yankees	(July 12 - 18)
Cats	(July 19 - 25)
The Sound of Music	(July 26 - August 1)
Footloose	(August 2 - 8)
Show Boat	(August 9 - 15)

2011
Legally Blonde	(June 20 - 26)
Kiss Me, Kate	(June 27 - July 3)
The Little Mermaid	(July 6 - 14)
Singin' in the Rain	(July 18 - 24)
Little Shop of Horrors	(July 25 - 31)
Seven Brides for Seven Brothers	(August 1 - 7)
Bye Bye Birdie	(August 8 - 14)

2012
Thoroughly Modern Millie	(June 18 - 24)
Chicago	(June 25 - July 1)
Aladdin	(July 5 - 13)
Dreamgirls	(July 16 - 22)
Joseph and the Amazing Technicolor® Dreamcoat	(July 23 - 29)
Pirates! (or, Gilbert & Sullivan Plunder'd)	(July 30 - August 5)
The King and I	(August 6 - 12)

2013
Spamalot	(June 17 - 23)
Shrek the Musical	(June 24 - 30)
Nunsense - Muny Style!	(July 1 - 7)
South Pacific	(July 8 - 14)
Les Misérables	(July 15 - 21)
Mary Poppins the Musical	(July 25 - August 2)
West Side Story	(August 5 - 11)

2014
Billy Elliot	(June 16 - 22)
Tarzan	(June 25 - July 2)
Porgy and Bess	(July 7 - 13)
The Addams Family	(July 14 - 20)
Seussical	(July 22 - 28)
Grease	(July 31 - August 8)
Hello, Dolly!	(August 11 - 17)

2015
My Fair Lady	(June 15 - 21)
Hairspray	(June 23 - 30)
Holiday Inn	(July 6 - 12)
Buddy: The Buddy Holly Story	(July 13 - 19)
Into the Woods	(July 21 - 27)
Beauty and the Beast	(July 29 - August 7)
Oklahoma!	(August 10 - 16)

2016
The Wizard of Oz	(June 13 - 2)
42nd Street	(June 24 - 30)
The Music Man	(July 5 - 11)
Young Frankenstein	(July 13 - 19)
Mamma Mia!	(July 21 - 28)
Fiddler on the Roof	(July 30 - August 5)
Aida (Elton John and Tim Rice)	(August 8 - 14)

2017
Jesus Christ Superstar	(June 12 - 18)
The Little Mermaid	(June 20 - 29)
A Funny Thing Happened on the Way to the Forum	(July 5 - 11)
All Shook Up	(July 13 - 19)
The Unsinkable Molly Brown	(July 21 - 17)
A Chorus Line	(July 29 - August 4)
Newsies the Musical	(August 7 - 13)

2018
Jerome Robbins' Broadway	(June 11 - 17)
The Wiz	(June 19 - 25)
Singin' In the Rain	(June 27 - July 3)
Jersey Boys	(July 9 - 16)
Annie	(July 19 - 25)
Gypsy	(July 27 - August 2)
Meet Me In St. Louis	(August 4 - 12)

Mike Isaacson, 2011

At the end of the 2011 season, Paul Blake retired from The Muny, and his successor, Mike Isaacson was named.

" I almost talked myself out of this. When Denny first called in anticipation of Paul's departure, I helped him brainstorm candidates. 'What if you did it?' he finally asked. I told him that if he wanted someone to continue doing exactly what The Muny was already doing, I wasn't the right person. He said The Muny definitely wanted to start a new chapter but wasn't yet sure what shape it would take. So I quietly began seeing and analyzing every show, studying every audience, reviewing the arc of nine decades.

"It didn't take long for me to realize that this was one of the great theatres of the world; a national treasure; and a citadel of St. Louis spirit. Nonetheless, I felt that The Muny needed a new quality of production, one that would excite and engage and surprise the audience in a way that wasn't happening. The Muny needed to become a metaphor of St. Louis's ability to create work that would stand up against any other theatre, anywhere on the globe. The bottomless love, respect, loyalty and devotion that the Muny audience had bestowed over five generations needed to be renewed, and the phrase 'Alone in Its Greatness' needed to feel absolutely real and alive today, instead of merely bookmarking our glorious artistic and civic past. And so, in the spring of 2011, I began. I offer no opinion about whether I've succeeded; that's for the future to decide. For me, all that matters is what are we creating, right here, right now. "

Mike Isaacson
Artistic Director and
Executive Producer

The LED Wall, 2012

Prior to 2012, a backdrop called "the sky truck" spanned the back of the stage, lending a generic mask to the upstage area. Mike Isaccson had an LED wall installed in 2012, allowing for dramatic and intricate stage pictures at the touch of a button.

LEFT: The LED wall took audiences "under the sea," with *The Little Mermaid,* 2017.

" 20 feet high, 25 wide, and 6 feet deep, the scenery wall weighs just under 1,200 pounds. It is made up of panels, and each panel is made up of 16 modules. A single module has 1,736 LEDs. Those lights can create 185 trillion color combinations..

"The scenic designers will use the LEDs to create patterns — for example, a sunset over the water for *Pirates! (or Gilbert & Sullivan Plunder'd)* or blaring tabloid headlines for "*Chicago.*"

Judith Newmark,
St. Louis Post-Dispatch, April 29, 2012

RIGHT: An LED-generated montage of vintage theatre marquees served as a backdrop for 42ND STREET, 2016

"Whale Fin" Fans, 2012

Photo by Phillip Hamer

The original fans were first installed in the auditorium in 1955. Although effective during pre-show and at intermission, they were too loud to run during the show. By 2012, "whale fin" technology allowed the fans to run as silently as whales swim. Muny audiences can now enjoy an appreciable breeze throughout the evening.

Photo by Phillip Hamer

This close-up of the fan blades show their slightly curved surface and the serrated edges that allow them to function soundlessly.

MARY POPPINS, 2013

Disney magic met Muny magic, when Mary Poppins flew over the audience. Executive producer Mike Isaacson pointed out that while there had been Muny flights before, all had taken place over the stage. Jenny Powers played the practically perfect nanny.

Mary Poppins will sail over the Muny

With special effect, actress Jenny Powers will 'fly' over the audience, not just the stage this summer.

BY JUDITH NEWMARK
jnewmark@post-dispatch.com
314-340-8243

This summer at the Muny, Mary Poppins will fly over the audience.

It will make Muny history, executive producer Mike Isaacson pointed out. There have been Muny flights before – for example, in 1967's "It's a Bird . . . It's a Plane . . . It's Superman" and, of course, in many productions of "Peter Pan." But all those "flights" took place over the stage.

ZFX, a company that specializes in stage flight, will create the special effect. "They promise to take the Muny audience to new heights," Isaacson said, "which is something we've taken rather literally."

Jenny Powers will take wing as the title character in Disney and Cameron Mackintosh's "Mary Poppins the Musical." She is currently starring in New York in the Irish Rep's production of "Donnybrook!"; recently, she had another flight-related role,

playing Lois Lane in a revival of "It's a Bird . . ." at Encores!

Rob McClure will co-star as Bert, a dancing chimney sweep. He is nominated for the 2013 Tony Award for leading actor in a musical for his performance in the title role in "Chaplin the Musical."

Stephen Buntrock, who made his Muny debut last season starring in "Thoroughly Modern Millie," and his real-life wife, Erin Dilly, will play Mr. and Mrs. Banks, the couple who hire a flying governess. Their

children, Jane and Michael Banks, will be played by Elizabeth Teeter and Aidan Gemme, who played Jane and Michael on Broadway. Elizabeth Teeter, a St. Louisan, has played many roles at theaters around town, including Flounder in "The Little Mermaid" at the Muny.

Gary Griffin will direct "Mary Poppins," and Alex Sanchez is the choreographer.

"Mary Poppins" will run from July 25 to Aug. 2. Subscribers will have their regular seats from July 25 to 31. The

two "extra" performances – usual for the Muny's children's show – have no subscription seats. That means seats that are usually not available for single ticket sales, or for group sales, will be available at those shows. Group ticket sales are underway; single tickets go on sale June 1. For more information, call the box office at at 314-301-1900, or visit muny.org.

Judith Newmark is the Post-Dispatch theater critic. Follow her on Twitter @judithnewmark.

Photo by Phillip Hamer

A Few Leading Ladies

The 2010s – and Mike Isaccson – brought a host of new performers to the Muny stage .

From The Muny Archive

Jennifer Holliday, 2012

Jennifer Holiday recreated her iconic performance as Effie, in The Muny's 2012 production of *Dreamgirls*.

Photo by Phillip Hamer

Phyllis Smith, 2013

Native St. Louisan and star of television's *The Office* gloried in her role of Sister Julia, Child of God, in *Nunsense Muny Style!* (2013). The character was custom designed by *Nunsense* author Dan Goggin.

Heather Headley, 2015

After an eight-year hiatus from the American stage, Heather Headley enchanted Muny audiences as The Witch in *Into the Woods* (2015).

Photo by Phillip Hamer

A Few Leading Men

Ben Davis, 2013

Ben Davis made his Muny debut in *South Pacific* and quickly became a Muny favorite. Here he is as Curly with Christine Cornish Smith in *Oklahoma!* (2015).

Photo by Phillip Hamer

Photo by Phillip Hamer

Rob McClure, 2013

Rob McClure's Lord Farquaad in *Shrek* was just one of seven (and counting!) memorable Muny roles played by this versatile performer.

Norm Lewis, 2013

Norm Lewis almost had audiences rooting for the "bad guy" when he played Javert in *Les Misérables*.

From The Muny Archive

PETER MESSINEO
CHORUS BOY TO COSTUME COORDINATOR

Peter Messineo began his Muny career in 1949 in the men's ensemble. He retired from The Muny stage in 1958, segueing into stage management. In 1961, he moved into the costume department, and continued working there through the 2012 season.

From the Peter Messineo Collection

"So many memories, so many friendships, so many wonderful years, all because of the privilege of being associated with the wonderful theatre in Forest Park — The Muny!

"I was a freshman at St. Louis University High, and the memory of the shows I'd seen at The Muny as a child prompted me to audition for the chorus. I cut classes, but unfortunately, my rendition of 'The Desert Song' didn't get me chosen. I was told to come back next year, when my voice had changed.

"Of course, I did just that. I returned, and returned, and returned again, always with 'The Desert Song' in hand. Finally, in 1949, I was chosen to be in the chorus — naturally, after a rousing rendition of 'The Desert Song.' It was so exciting to be in the singing ensemble! There were 22 singing men, 20 singing women, nine dancing men and 17 dancing women. We did 11 shows, one following the other, for a total of 12 and-a-half weeks.

"This meant a lot of rehearsals and a lot of show, but we didn't mind the work; after all, we were part of the wonderful Muny family.

From The Muny Archive

"As the years followed, I became a stage manager, which led to wardrobe master, from there to head of the wardrobe department, and eventually costume coordinator.

"The years have passed — many friendships made and treasured. But the treasure of them all is the opportunity I was given to be associated with the family of the spectacular Muny. For that I will always be grateful!"

Peter Messineo

From The Muny Archive

MUNY MAGIC AT THE SHELDON

Muny Associate Producer Megan Larche Dominick produced a series of intimate concerts starring some of The Muny's favorite performers. The Sheldon Concert Hall, famous for its perfect acoustics, was chosen as the venue.

BETH LEAVEL

Muny Magic at the Sheldon: Beth Leavel (November 11 and 12, 2015)

A Night with the Buddy Holly Boys (April 13 and 14, 2016)
Starring Andy Christopher, Joe Cosmo Cogen, Kyle Lacy and Nathan Yates Douglas

Today's Muny Stars Salute the Legends (November 16 and 17, 2016)
Starring Danielle Bowen, Ali Ewoldt, Stephanie Gibson and Elena Shaddow

My 70s Show! A Night with Nicholas Rodriguez (March 29 and 30, 2017)

Our Leading Men (October 18 and 19, 2017)
Ben Davis, Davis Gaines, Jay Armstrong Johnson and Mykal Kilgore

Muny Magic at the Sheldon: Laura Michelle Kelly (March 21 and 22, 2018)
Note: The March 22 show was canceled due to illness.

Photo by Phillip Hamer

NANCY FREER SHERWIN
DIRECTOR OF YOUTH PROGRAMS

Photo by David Stone

Nancy Freer Sherwin is the Director of Youth Programs. Her areas of influence include Muny Kids, Muny Teens, and The Muny's outreach and educational programs: Make a Musical, Acting for Musical Theatre, and the St. Louis High School Musical Theatre Awards.

From the Nancy Freer Sherwin collection

"My first memory of The Muny is watching *Peter Pan* and asking my dad, "How do they get to do that?" Thus began a life-long love of musical theatre and The Muny. I performed for a number of years in the children's chorus, beginning with *The Wizard of Oz* featuring Margaret Hamilton as the Witch.

"The Muny always felt like home, and I returned as an adult, sometimes as a performer and sometimes as a season-ticket holder. My current position offers the opportunity to share my passion for musical theatre and The Muny with future generations."

Nancy Freer Sherwin

The photo ABOVE is from The Muny's 1958 production of *Show Boat*. Margaret Hamilton starred as Parthy Ann. With her (clockwise from upper right) are Martha Freer, Nancy Freer Sherwin and Temple Kelleher.

THE MUNY TEENS

MAKE A MUSICAL

Photo by Phillip Hamer

THE LAST WORD

It's not easy to think of The Muny in terms of History. It is — and always has been — a living, breathing entity. When our files became our archive, it was a bit jarring, because we use those files every day in the sometimes frenetic business of putting on a summer season of musicals for St. Louis.

The 2018 Centennial Season taught all of us that while our history is unique and specific to its time and place, and while that history tells a series of fascinating and interconnected stories, the value of that history is not to immortalize the past.

Rather, we have come to see our past an unbroken line to the future. We speak of an institution having a cultural identity, a heritage based on the standards and traditions it has created through the years. The Muny's identity is emphatic, clear-cut, and easily understood.

We are, and always have been, a theatre experience designed to please the people we serve: The people of St. Louis. We have always tried to choose the shows, the actors, the sets, costumes and designs that will speak to our audience. We have always made it our mission to be accessible to all, physically and financially.

While we celebrate the past in our 100th Season in Forest Park, we are looking ahead to the future. We are literally planting trees that we will not live to see in their full growth. But our children, and grandchildren, and generations beyond will.

It seems fitting, then, to close this chapter of the story
not with "The End," but rather with
"To Be Continued."

Denny Reagan
President & CEO

Architect's rendering of the majestic new Muny stage, slated to debut in 2019.

98653326R00064

Made in the USA
Lexington, KY
09 September 2018